Table of Contents

 MATH SERIES

by Stan VerNooy

Book cover design by Kathy Kifer

Dedicated to

Lonnie Meegan	Katia Waff
Michelle Poore	Wade Fox
Pamela Bereman	Alison Willis
Stephanie Ryan	Dianne Williams
Laura Locher	Maria Eckholt

Published by
Garlic Press
605 Powers St.
Eugene, OR 97402

ISBN: 978-0-931993-64-0
Order Number GP-064
Printed in China

www.garlicpress.com

Introduction to Calculus AB

The two volumes of **Straight Forward Calculus AB** are intended to cover all material in a standard high school Advanced Placement Calculus AB course. The overall format of the books provides explanations of specific topics, followed by example(s) modeling the topics, and exercises to reinforce proficiency of the presented topics. It is assumed that the reader is familiar with the material in the algebra, trigonometry, and pre-calculus books of the **Straight Forward Series**.

Calculus AB includes the elements of differential and integral calculus of functions of a single variable, including standard applications such as optimization, related rates, volumes of solids of rotation, and separable differential equations. The rigorous theoretical foundations of calculus, such as the delta-epsilon definition of a limit, are not covered. Those more rigorous topics are left to Calculus BC.

Limits & Continuity

Calculus is based entirely on functions. An understanding of the facts in this section is required before proceeding to the rest of the topics in this book. This material was presented in greater detail in **Straight Forward Pre-Calculus**.

The **domain** of a function is the set of all numbers which can legally be used as input to the function. If the function is described as f(x) = (some formula involving x), then the domain is the set of all legal values of x.

The **range** of a function is the set of all numbers which can possibly be the output of the function; in other words, the set of all possible values of f(x).

The **sum, product, difference,** and **quotient** of two functions f(x) and g(x) are exactly what you would expect: the sum is f(x) + g(x), the difference is f(x) - g(x), the product is f(x)g(x), and the quotient is $\frac{f(x)}{g(x)}$.

The **composition** of two functions f(x) and g(x) is the function obtained by using the output of g(x) as the input to f(x); in functional notation, the composition is f(g(x)). The two functions can also be composed in the reverse order as g(f(x)), and the two compositions are NOT the same.

The functions f(x) and g(x) are **inverses** of (or to) each other if f(g(x)) = x, and g(f(x)) = x. Informally, each function *undoes* what the other function does.

A function f is **even** if f(-x) = f(x) for all x in the domain of f. A function g is **odd** if g(-x) = -g(x) for all x in the domain of g.

A function f is **periodic** if there is a positive number p such that f(x+p) = f(x) for all x in the domain of f. If p is the smallest positive value for which f(x+p) always equals f(x), then p is the **period** of f. Informally, a periodic function always repeats itself at intervals of length p.

The **zeros** of a function f(x) are the values of x in the domain of f, such that f(x) = 0.

A **y-intercept** of a graph is any point at which the graph intersects the y-axis. The x-coordinate of a y-intercept is always zero. Thus, if the graph is of a function f(x), then there is at most one y-intercept; namely, f(0).

An **x-intercept** of a graph is any point at which the graph intersects the x-axis. The y-coordinate of an x-intercept is always zero. Thus, if the graph is of a function, then the x-intercepts occur at all the zeros of the function.

A graph is **symmetrical with respect to the y-axis** if, when you fold the graph along the y-axis, the left and right halves of the graph coincide. If the graph is of a function, then it is symmetrical with respect to the y-axis if and only if the function is even. If the graph is of an equation (whether or not the equation describes a function), then it is symmetrical with respect to the y-axis if and only if you can substitute -x for every occurrence of x in the equation, and end up with an equation equivalent to the original.

A graph is **symmetrical with respect to the origin** if you can spin the graph 180 degrees around the origin and end up with the same graph you started with. If the graph is of a function, then the graph is symmetrical with respect to the origin if and only if the function is odd. If the graph is of an equation (whether or not the equation describes a function), then it is symmetrical with respect to the origin if and only if you can substitute -x for every occurrence of x in the equation __and__ -y for every occurrence of y, and end up with an equation equivalent to the original.

If you begin with a graph of y = f(x), then there are some changes you can make to the equation or to the function which will result in predictable changes to the graph. The rules for these graph transformations follow:

Change y = f(x) to:	Make this change to the graph:
y = kf(x) (k > 1)	Stretch vertically by a factor of k.
y = kf(x) (0 < k < 1)	Shrink vertically by a factor of k.
y = -f(x)	Reflect in x-axis (up and down).
y = f(x)+k (or y - k = f (x))	Shift up k units.
y = f(x)-k (or y+k = f(x))	Shift down k units.
y = f(kx) (k > 1)	Shrink horizontally by a factor of $\frac{1}{k}$.
y = f(kx) (0 < k < 1)	Stretch horizontally by a factor of $\frac{1}{k}$.
y = f(x+k)	Shift left by k units.
y = f(x-k)	Shift right by k units.
y = f(-x)	Reflect in y-axis (left and right).

$y = |f(x)|$

Reflect everything below the x-axis across the x-axis to the upper half of the graph.

$y = f(|x|)$

Delete the part of the graph to the left of the y-axis, then replace that part with a mirror image of the right-hand half:

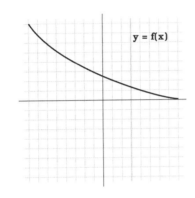

y = f(x)

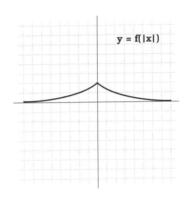

y = f(|x|)

Limits and Continuity. Exercise 1. Review of Function Properties.

For problems 1-16, let:

$$f(x) = 3 - \sqrt{2x + 5}$$
$$g(x) = \frac{4-x}{2x^2 - 5x - 42}$$
$$k(x) = 7x - 4$$
$$j(x) = \frac{3x-2}{2x+3}$$

1. Find the domains of f(x), g(x), k(x), and j(x).
2. Find the ranges of f(x) and k(x).
3. Find (k+j)(x) and simplify.
4. Find $(\frac{j}{g})(x)$.
5. Find (fg)(x).
6. Find j(k(x)) and simplify.
7. Find k(j(x)) and simplify.
8. Find j(7x) - 4 and simplify.

9. Find 7j(x) - 4 and simplify.

10. Find 7j(x-4) and simplify.

11. Find f(x+h).

12. Find $j^{-1}(x)$.

13. Find the zeros of f(x), g(x), k(x), and j(x).

14. Find the y-intercepts of f(x), g(x), k(x), and j(x).

15. Find the x-intercepts of f(x), g(x), k(x), and j(x).

16. Find $\frac{j(x+h)-j(x)}{h}$ and simplify.

17. Identify each function below as even, odd, both, or neither.

   a. $f_1(x) = \frac{x^2+2}{x^4-5}$ c. $f_3(x) = 2x^5 + 6x$

   b. $f_2(x) = 0$ d. $f_4(x) = 2x^5 + 6$

18. Given this graph, draw the graphs of:

   a. f(x+1)
   b. f(x)+1
   c. f(-x)
   d. -f(x)
   e. f(-3x)
   f. -3f(x)
   g. |f(x)|
   h. f(|x|)
   i. f(3-x)-4

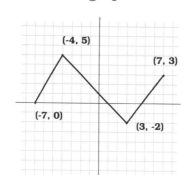

Part 2

The Meaning of Limits

The "limit of f(x) as x goes to 5", denoted by **lim** f(x), is the value which f(x)
                                                    x→5
gets close to, as x gets close to 5. Often, this limit is just f(5), but it isn't
always!

4

•Examples:

1. Let f(x) = x - 3. We examine what happens to f(x) as x gets closer and closer to 5. By doing the calculations, we construct this table:

x	f(x)
4.9	1.9
4.99	1.99
4.999	1.999
5.1	2.1
5.01	2.01
5.001	2.001

We can see from the table that, as x gets close to 5, f(x) is getting close to 2. Therefore, we say that $\lim_{x \to 5} f(x) = 2$.

Notice that we never calculated f(5) itself! It is true that f(5) is equal to 2, but that has nothing to do with the limit.

2. If $g(x) = \frac{x^2 - 8x + 15}{x - 5}$, then g(5) is not defined (because 5 is not in the domain of g(x)). However, if we calculate the values of g(x) for the same values of x which we used in Example 1, we would construct the exact same table as in that example. Therefore, $\lim_{x \to 5} g(x) = 2$.

3. Suppose $h(x) = \begin{cases} x - 3 & x < 5 \\ x + 7 & x = 5 \\ x - 3 & x > 5 \end{cases}$.

In this case, h(5) = 12, so h(5) is defined. But a table of values of h(x) for x values close to 5 would once again produce the exact same table as in Example 1. Therefore, once again, $\lim_{x \to 5} g(x) = 2$.

4. Let $f(x) = \begin{cases} x + 1 & x < 4.995 \\ x - 3 & 4.995 \leq x \leq 5.005 \\ 2x^3 & 5.005 < x \end{cases}$.

In this case, f(4.99) and f(5.01) are not close to 2. But if we take x values even closer to 5—in particular from the interval (4.995, 5.005)—then we will find that f(x) approaches 2 again:

x	f(x)
4.996	1.996
4.999	1.999
4.9999	1.9999
5.004	2.004
5.001	2.001
5.0001	2.0001

Once again, $\lim_{x \to 5} g(x) = 2$.

IMPORTANT FACT:

Examples 2 and 3 demonstrate that $\lim\limits_{x \to 5} f(x)$ might not have anything at all to do with f(5)!

Needless to say, the number 5 is not special. The exact same approach would be used to find $\lim\limits_{x \to 6} f(x)$, $\lim\limits_{x \to -\frac{1}{2}} f(x)$, or $\lim\limits_{x \to 0} f(x)$.

Using Graphs to Determine Limits

Remember that if the point (a, b) is on the graph of y = f(x), then b = f(a). So if we want to determine $\lim\limits_{x \to -3} f(x)$ from the graph of f(x), we look for the <u>y</u>-coordinate of the point the graph seems to be approaching as <u>x</u> approaches -3.

•Examples:

All three graphs below approach the point (-3,1) as x approaches -3. It is true that the point (-3, 1) is not actually on the second or third graph, which means that g(-3) and h(-3) are not equal to 1: g(-3) is undefined, and h(-3) = 5. But that has nothing to do with the limit as x goes to -3! The graphs show us that $\lim\limits_{x \to -3} f(x)$, $\lim\limits_{x \to -3} g(x)$, and $\lim\limits_{x \to -3} h(x)$ are all equal to 1.

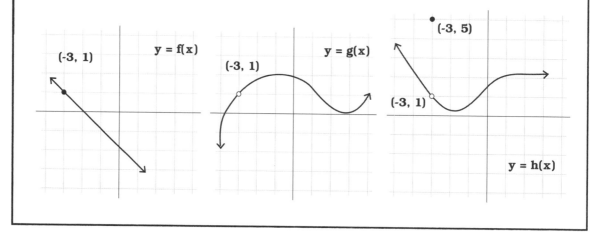

BIG-TIME WARNING

$\lim\limits_{x \to -c} f(x)$ doesn't have to exist at all! All examples so far have dealt with limits which do exist, but we will see in a subsequent section that there are several reasons why a desired limit might be undefined.

Limits and Continuity. Exercise 2. The Meaning of Limits.

1. Find $\lim\limits_{x \to 2} (3x + 4)$.

2. Find $\lim\limits_{x \to -2} \frac{x^2+5}{1-x}$.

3. Find $\lim\limits_{x \to 0} \frac{x^2+2x}{x}$.

4. Find $\lim\limits_{x \to 3} \frac{x^2+2x}{x}$.

5. Find $\lim\limits_{x \to 1} f(x)$, where

$$f(x) = \begin{cases} x + 3 & x < -1 \\ 5 - x & -1 \le x \le 3 \\ \sqrt{x+15} & 3 < x \end{cases}$$

6. Find $\lim\limits_{x \to 1} g(x)$, where

$$g(x) = \begin{cases} x + 3 & x < 1 \\ \sqrt{x+15} & 1 < x \end{cases}$$

7. Find $\lim\limits_{x \to 1} h(x)$ <u>and</u> $h(1)$, where

$$h(x) = \begin{cases} x + 3 & x < 1 \\ \sqrt{\pi} & x = 1 \\ \sqrt{x+15} & 1 < x \end{cases}$$

8. Find $\lim\limits_{x \to 1} f(x)$, where

$$f(x) = \begin{cases} 23x - 8 & x < 0.99 \\ x - 5 & 0.99 \le x \le 1.01 \\ 8 - 23x & 1.01 < x \end{cases}$$

9. Find $\lim\limits_{x \to -3}$ of the function
   in this graph:

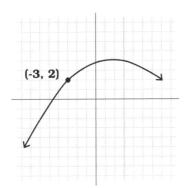

10. Find $\lim\limits_{x \to 3}$ of the function
    in this graph:

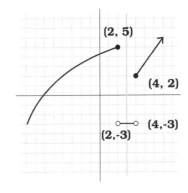

Part 3

One-Sided Limits

In the previous section, we determined $\lim\limits_{x \to 5} f(x)$ by looking at the value of f(x) when x was slightly less than 5 <u>and</u> when x was slightly greater than 5. Looking back at Example 1, page 5, we see that f(x) is getting close to 2 when x approaches 5 from below, and f(x) gets close to the same number (2) as x approaches 5 from above.

Suppose, instead, that we have a function whose value approaches 2 as x gets close to 5 from below, but approaches some other number, such as -3, as x gets close to 5 from above. In that case, $\lim\limits_{x \to 5} f(x)$ would not exist at all.

However, there is a sort of "half limit", or, more commonly, <u>one-sided</u> limit, which tells us the value which f(x) approaches as x gets close to 5 <u>only from above</u>, or <u>only from below</u>. The limit of f(x) as x approaches 5 from below is called the <u>left-hand limit</u>, and is denoted $\lim\limits_{x \to 5^-} f(x)$. The limit of f(x) as x approaches 5 from above is called right-hand limit and is denoted $\lim\limits_{x \to 5^+} f(x)$.

The reason for the terminology is that on the xy-plane, approaching 5 from below means approaching 5 from the left.

•Examples:

1. Let $f(x) = \begin{cases} 2x + 1 & x < 5 \\ \sqrt{x + 4} & 5 \le x \end{cases}$.

If we constuct a table of values for f(x) when x is slightly less than 5, we get the following:

x	f(x)
4.099	10.98
4.999	10.998
4.9999	10.9998

From the table, we conclude reasonably (and correctly!) that $\lim\limits_{x \to 5^-} f(x) = 11$.

A similar table for values of x slightly greater than 5 would look like this:

x	f(x)
5.01	3.001666
5.001	3.000167
5.0001	3.000017

From the table, we conclude that $\lim\limits_{x \to 5^+} f(x) = 3$. Notice that f(5) = 3, but that is an irrelevant fact in determining left-hand and right-hand limits, just as it was irrelevant in the previous section.

2. Let $g(x) = \begin{cases} 2x+1 & x < 5 \\ \sqrt{x+4} & 5 < x \end{cases}$.

In this case, g(5) is not even defined. But an examination of the behavior of g(x) as x approaches 5 from below or above will give us the exact same tables of values we had in Example 1 above. Therefore, $\lim\limits_{x \to 5^-} g(x) = 11$, and $\lim\limits_{x \to 5^+} g(x) = 3$, just as in Example 1.

3. Finally, let $k(x) = \begin{cases} 2x+1 & x < 5 \\ 98.6 & x = 5 \\ \sqrt{x+4} & 5 < x \end{cases}$.

In this case, k(5) = 98.6. However, that is once again an irrelevant fact when it comes to computing limits. If we examine the behavior of k(x) when x is <u>close</u> to 5 from below, and <u>close</u> to 5 from above, we can again construct tables identical to those in Example 1. Thus, once again $\lim\limits_{x \to 5^-} k(x) = 11$, and $\lim\limits_{x \to 5^+} k(x) = 3$.

The Relationship Between $\lim\limits_{x \to c} f(x)$, and $\lim\limits_{x \to c^-} f(x)$, and $\lim\limits_{x \to c^+} f(x)$.

If c is any number, then $\lim\limits_{x \to c} f(x)$ exists only if

$$\lim\limits_{x \to c^+} f(x) = \lim\limits_{x \to c^-} f(x).$$

If $\lim\limits_{x \to c^-} f(x)$ and $\lim\limits_{x \to c^+} f(x)$ are equal, then

$$\lim\limits_{x \to c} f(x) = \lim\limits_{x \to c^+} f(x) = \lim\limits_{x \to c^-} f(x).$$

In the three examples above, $\lim\limits_{x \to 5} f(x)$, $\lim\limits_{x \to 5} g(x)$, $\lim\limits_{x \to 5} k(x)$ do not exist, because their left-hand limits at 5 are not equal to their right-hand limits at 5.

Finding One-Sided Limits from Graphs.

The procedure for determining a left-hand or right-hand limit from a graph is the same as determining a regular (two-sided) limit, except that we look only on the left or only on the right of the x-value we are interested in.

Examples:

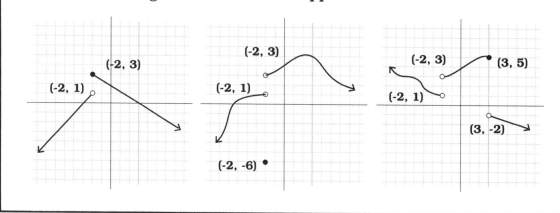

In all three of the graphs below, the left-hand limit as x approaches -2 is 1, and the right-hand limit as x approaches -2 is 3.

Limits and Continuity. Exercise 3. One-sided Limits.

In problems 1-8, find $\lim\limits_{x \to 2^-} f(x)$, $\lim\limits_{x \to 2^+} f(x)$, and $\lim\limits_{x \to 2} f(x)$.

1. $f(x) = \begin{cases} x^2 - x - 1 & x < 2 \\ x - 1 & 2 \le x \end{cases}$

2. $f(x) = \begin{cases} x^2 - x - 1 & x < 2 \\ x - 1 & 2 < x \end{cases}$

3. $f(x) = \begin{cases} x^2 - x - 1 & x < 2 \\ 86x + 5 & x = 2 \\ 2x - 3 & 2 < x \end{cases}$

4. $f(x) = \begin{cases} x^2 - x - 1 & x \le 2 \\ x + 1 & x > 2 \end{cases}$

5. $f(x) = \begin{cases} x + 1 & x \le 1.99 \\ \frac{x^2 - 4}{x - 2} & 1.99 < x < 2.01 \\ x - 1 & 2.01 \le x \end{cases}$

6. $f(x) = \begin{cases} 5 & x < 2 \\ 6 & 2 \le x \end{cases}$

7. $f(x) = \begin{cases} 5 & x < 2 \\ 6 & 2 < x \end{cases}$

8. $f(x) = \begin{cases} 5 & x < 2 \\ 7 & x = 2 \\ 6 & 2 < x \end{cases}$

In problems 9 - 12, find $\lim\limits_{x \to -4^-}$, $\lim\limits_{x \to -4^+}$, and $\lim\limits_{x \to -4}$ for the function graphed.

9.

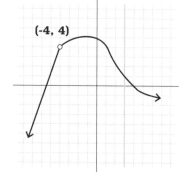

(-4, 4)

10.

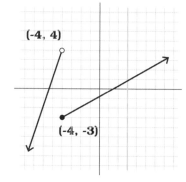

(-4, 4)

(-4, -3)

11.

(-2, 4)
(-5, 4)
(-5,-2) (-2,-2)

12.

(-4, 4)
(-4, 2)
(-4,-3)

Part 4 | **Limits at Infinity**

In the previous sections we examined the values of a function f(x) as x approached a specified number. In this section we look at what happens to the values of f(x) as x gets either huge and positive, or huge and negative.

Many functions, such as $7x + 18 - 5x^2$, have huge values when x is huge, so that there is no specific limit as x approaches plus or minus infinity. However, consider the following:

•Example:

$f(x) = \frac{4x-7}{x+3}$.

If we substitute progressively larger values for x into this function, we can construct a table similar to the ones in the previous sections.

x	f(x)
999	3.9810379
10,000	3.9981006
99,999	3.9998100
1,000,000	3.9999810

From the information in the table, we conclude that as x gets huge, the value of the function is approaching 4. In mathematical notation, that means:
$$\lim_{x \to \infty} f(x) = 4 .$$

If we substitute successively larger negative numbers into f(x), we can construct a similar table:

x	f(x)
-999	3.9810379
-10,000	3.9981006
-99,999	3.9998100
-1,000,000	3.9999810

This table shows that the limit as x approaches negative infinity is also 4 —i.e., $\lim_{x \to -\infty} f(x) = 4$.

There is an algebraic procedure which can be used to determine limits of a rational function as x approaches plus or minus infinity:

First, we divide every term in both the numerator and the denominator by the highest power of x which appears anywhere in the function.

Second, we note that a fraction with a number on top and a power of x on the bottom (such as $\frac{-3}{x^2}$), will approach zero as x gets huge positive or huge negative. Therefore, we drop each such term from the numerator and the denominator. If a number is left over, then that number is the limit of the function as x approaches plus or minus infinity.

•Examples:

1. Use the method described above to calculate $\lim\limits_{x \to \infty} \frac{4x+7}{x-3}$ and $\lim\limits_{x \to -\infty} \frac{4x+7}{x-3}$.

   The highest power of x in the function is x itself. When we divide each term in the numerator and denominator by x, we get:

   $$\frac{\frac{4x}{x}+\frac{7}{x}}{\frac{x}{x}-\frac{3}{x}} = \frac{4+\frac{7}{x}}{1-\frac{3}{x}}$$

   Then drop $\frac{7}{x}$ and $\frac{3}{x}$ from the function, since both of them approach zero as x gets huge. That leaves us with $\frac{4}{1}$, which shows that $\lim\limits_{x \to \infty} \frac{4x+7}{x-3} = 4$, and $\lim\limits_{x \to -\infty} \frac{4x+7}{x-3} = 4$.

2. Find $\lim\limits_{x \to \infty} \frac{4x+7}{x^2-3}$.

   In this case x^2 is the highest power of x in the function. So we divide each term in the numerator and denominator by x^2 , and we get:

   $$\frac{\frac{4x}{x^2}+\frac{7}{x^2}}{\frac{x^2}{x^2}-\frac{3}{x}} = \frac{\frac{4}{x}+\frac{7}{x^2}}{1-\frac{3}{x^2}}$$

   Now we drop the terms $\frac{4}{x}$, $\frac{7}{x^2}$, and $\frac{3}{x^2}$, because they all approach zero as x gets huge. That leaves us with nothing at all on top, and 1 on the bottom. Therefore, the limit is <u>zero</u>:

   $$\lim\limits_{x \to \infty} \frac{4x+7}{x^2-3} = 0.$$

3. Find $\lim\limits_{x \to \infty} \dfrac{4x^2+7x-2}{x-3}$.

Once again, x^2 is the highest power of x in the function. So we divide every term on the top and bottom by x^2. The result is:

$$\frac{\frac{4x^2}{x^2}+\frac{7x}{x^2}-\frac{2}{x^2}}{\frac{x}{x^2}-\frac{3}{x^2}} = \frac{4+\frac{7}{x}-\frac{2}{x^2}}{\frac{1}{x}-\frac{3}{x^2}}$$

This time, four of the five terms get dropped, leaving us with the number 4 on top, and zero on the bottom. This information tells us that the limit is <u>undefined</u>, because a denominator is not allowed to be zero.

More precisely, in this example the value of $\dfrac{4x^2+7x-2}{x-3}$ will increase or decrease beyond any limit as x approaches positive or negative infinity. We cannot tell from this method whether the value of f(x) is going in a positive or negative direction as x becomes huge positive; we know only that the value goes beyond any finite limit. By using the table we did at the beginning of this section, we can see more accurately what happens:

x	f(x)
999	4,015
10,000	40,019
99,999	400,015
1,000,000	4,000,019
-999	-3977
-10,000	-39,981
-99,999	-399,977
-1,000,000	-3,999,981

So the table show us that $\dfrac{4x^2+7x-2}{x-3}$ decreases to huge negative numbers as x approaches minus infinity, and increases to huge positive numbers as x approaches minus infinity.

Taken together, the examples above give us a quick procedure for finding the limits of rational functions as x approaches plus or minus infinity. First we look at the degree of the numerator and the degree of the denominator. Then we use the following rules:

1. If the degree of the numerator is less than the degree of the denominator, the limit as x goes to plus or minus infinity is zero.

2. If the degree of the numerator is greater than the degree of the denominator, the limit as x goes to plus or minus infinity is undefined.

3. If the degree of the numerator is equal to the degree of the denominator, then use the alegebraic procedure in the example above to find the limit. The limit as x approaches minus infinity will be the same as the limit as x approaches plus infinity.

13

Limits and Continuity. Exercise 4. Limits at Infinity.

Find each.

1. $\displaystyle\lim_{x\to\infty}\frac{4x^3-3x+1}{3x+1-2x^3}$

2. $\displaystyle\lim_{x\to-\infty}\frac{4x^3-3x+1}{3x+1-2x^3}$

3. $\displaystyle\lim_{x\to\infty}\frac{4x^3-3x+1}{\left|3x+1-2x^3\right|}$

4. $\displaystyle\lim_{x\to-\infty}\frac{4x^3-3x+1}{\left|3x+1-2x^3\right|}$

5. $\displaystyle\lim_{x\to\infty}\frac{4x^3-3x+1}{3x+1-2x^4}$

6. $\displaystyle\lim_{x\to-\infty}\frac{4x^4-3x+1}{3x+1-2x^3}$

7. $\displaystyle\lim_{x\to\infty}\frac{4x^3-3x+\sin x}{3x+1-2x^3}$

8. $\displaystyle\lim_{x\to-\infty}\frac{3x+\pi}{2x-e}$

Part 5 Nonexistent Limits

In the previous section we saw an example of a function whose limit did not exist as x approached positive or negative infinity. There are many other cases of perfectly respectable functions whose limits do not exist at certain values of x. In this section we show some reasons why that might happen.

Reason 1: The left-hand limit might not equal the right-hand limit.

•Example:

> Let $f(x) = \begin{cases} x-3 & x<5 \\ x+3 & x\geq 5 \end{cases}$.
>
> Then $\displaystyle\lim_{x\to5^-} f(x) = 2$, and $\displaystyle\lim_{x\to5^+} f(x) = 8$. Since the limit from the left is not the same as the limit on the right, $\displaystyle\lim_{x\to5} f(x)$ is undefined.

Reason 2: The function might increase or decrease beyond any limit as x approaches the number in question.

•Example:

> Let $g(x) = \tan^2 x$. Then $\displaystyle\lim_{x\to\frac{\pi}{2}} g(x)$ is undefined, because as x gets close to $\frac{\pi}{2}$, $\tan^2 x$ becomes huge. By "huge", we mean here that no matter how big a number we care to name, $\tan^2 x$ will get bigger than our number if we take an x value close enough to $\frac{\pi}{2}$.

Reason 3: The function value may bounce back and forth instead of approaching any particular number as x approaches the number in question.

•Example:

Let $f(x) = \begin{cases} 2 & \text{if x is rational.} \\ -7 & \text{if x is irrational.} \end{cases}$

(Recall [from **Straight Forward Pre-Calculus**] that a rational number is one which can be expressed as a fraction whose numerator and denominator are both integers, and an irrational number is one which cannot be expressed that way. $\sqrt{2}$ and π are examples of irrational numbers.)

This function, famous for its unpleasantness, is a commonly used example of a function which lacks most of the properties which we want functions to have. It is an interesting fact that the interval between any two unequal numbers contains both an infinite number of rational numbers <u>and</u> an infinite number of <u>ir</u>rational numbers. Therefore, no matter how close x is to 13, there will always be some values closer to 13 for which f(x) = 2, and some other values, also closer to 13, for which f(x) = -7. This situation prevents us from finding any limit at all for f(x) as x approaches 13.

Reason 4: The number in question may be in an interval which is outside the domain of the function.

•Example:

Let $g(x) = \sqrt{x-5}$.

If we try to calculate $\lim_{x \to 4} g(x)$, we find that g(x) has no values at all when x is close to 4, because the domain of g(x) is [5, ∞). Therefore, $\lim_{x \to 4} g(x)$ is undefined.

15

Limits and Continuity. Exercise 5. Nonexistent Limits.

Find the limits which exist. If the limit called for in the exercise does not exist, then specify one of the four following reasons:

   a. The left- and right-hand limits exist but do not agree.
   b. The function increases or decreases beyond any limit.
   c. The function values bounce back and forth as x approaches the number in question.
   d. The number in question is inside an interval on which the function is not defined.

1. $\lim\limits_{x \to \infty} \csc x$

2. $\lim\limits_{x \to -2} \dfrac{x+2}{|x+2|}$

3. $\lim\limits_{x \to \infty} \sin x$

4. $\lim\limits_{x \to 0.9} \begin{cases} x & x < 1 \\ x+1 & x > 1 \end{cases}$

5. $\lim\limits_{x \to \frac{\pi}{4}} \begin{cases} \sin x & x \le \frac{\pi}{4} \\ \cos x & x > \frac{\pi}{4} \end{cases}$

6. $\lim\limits_{x \to 2.6} e^{\ln x}$

7. $\lim\limits_{x \to \infty} e^{x-99}$

8. $\lim\limits_{x \to \pi} \begin{cases} \sin x & x < \pi \\ \cos x & x \ge \pi \end{cases}$

9. $\lim\limits_{x \to -1} \ln x$

10. $\lim\limits_{x \to 1} \begin{cases} x & x < 1 \\ x+1 & x > 1 \end{cases}$

11. $\lim\limits_{x \to 3\pi} \cos(\dfrac{1}{x-3\pi})$

12. $\lim\limits_{x \to 0} \begin{cases} \dfrac{x^2}{x} & x < 0 \\ \dfrac{x}{x^2+1} & x \ge 0 \end{cases}$

13. $\lim\limits_{x \to 3} \sqrt{5 - x^2}$

14. $\lim\limits_{x \to 3} \dfrac{x-3}{x^2-6x+9}$

Part 6 Continuity

In **Straight Forward Pre-Calculus**, a continuous function was defined as one whose graph could be drawn without lifting the pencil from the paper. Now that we have the notion of a limit, we can give a more precise definition of continuity.

> If c is a value in the domain of a function f(x), then f(x) is said to be <u>continuous at c</u> if $\lim\limits_{x \to c} f(x) = f(c)$.

There are two reasons why a function might <u>not</u> be continuous at c: the limit of f(x) as x approaches c might not exist; or, the limit might exist but might be different from f(c).

•Example:

Let $f(x) = \begin{cases} x-1 & x < -3 \\ 2x-1 & -3 \le x < 0 \\ x^2-1 & 0 < x < 2 \\ 5-x & 2 \le x < 6 \\ -0.99 & x = 6 \\ 2x-13 & 6 < x \end{cases}$

Decide whether f(x) is continuous at -3, 0, 2, and 6.

Solution:

$\lim\limits_{x \to -3^-} f(x) = -4$, but $\lim\limits_{x \to 3^+} f(x) = -7$; therefore $\lim\limits_{x \to 3} f(x)$ is undefined, and f(x) cannot be continuous at -3.

$\lim\limits_{x \to 0} f(x) = -1$, and $\lim\limits_{x \to 0} f(x) = -1$; therefore $\lim\limits_{x \to 0} f(x) = -1$; but f(0) is not defined. Therefore f(x) is not continuous at 0.

$\lim\limits_{x \to 2} f(x)$, $\lim\limits_{x \to 2} f(x)$, and f(2) are all equal to 3. Therefore f(x) is continuous at 2.

$\lim\limits_{x \to 6^-} f(x) = -1$, and $\lim\limits_{x \to 6^+} f(x) = -1$; therefore $\lim\limits_{x \to 6} f(x) = -1$. However, f(6) = -0.99. So f(x) is not continuous at 6.

Most of the functions we commonly deal with are continuous *most* of the time:

1. If two functions are continuous, then their sum, their difference, their product, and their composition (in either order) are continuous everywhere.

2. All polynomials are continuous everywhere.

3. Rational functions are continuous everywhere except at the zeros of the denominator.

4. Exponential functions are continuous everywhere.

5. A log function, to any base, is continuous on its entire domain (i.e., the interval $(0,\infty)$). In particular, the ln function is continuous on $(0,\infty)$.

6. All six trigonometric functions are continuous on their domains. For the sine and cosine functions, this means they are continuous for all real numbers. The tangent function is continuous on the intervals $(-\frac{\pi}{2},\frac{\pi}{2})$, $(\frac{\pi}{2},\frac{3\pi}{2})$, $(\frac{3\pi}{2},\frac{5\pi}{2})$, etc.

7. An nth root function is continuous on its domain. For example, if $f(x) = \sqrt{x}$, then f is continuous on $[0,\infty)$. If $g(x) = \sqrt[5]{x}$, then g is continuous on $(-\infty,\infty)$.

•Examples:

All of these functions are continuous everywhere:

$3x^2 + 7$ $(3x^2 + 7) \cos x$

$\sin x - \cos x$ $\dfrac{\sqrt[3]{x-1}}{3x^2+7}$

e^{3x^2+7}

All of these functions are continuous except at 3 and -3:

$$\dfrac{3x^2+7}{x^2-9}, \quad \dfrac{e^x}{x+3} - \dfrac{\sin x}{x-3}, \quad \dfrac{\sin(7-x)}{x^4-18x^2+81}.$$

The function $\dfrac{e^{3x}}{\sin x}$ is continuous everywhere except at integer multiples of π.

The function $\tan(x^2+1)$ is continuous everywhere except where $x = \sqrt{\dfrac{n\pi-2}{2}}$, where n is an odd integer (WHY ?)

Continuity comes in several other flavors in addition to continuity at a particular point. Some of those others are described below.

f(x) is <u>left continuous at c</u> if $\lim\limits_{x \to c^-} f(x) = f(c)$.

f(x) is <u>right continuous at c</u> if $\lim\limits_{x \to c^+} f(x) = f(c)$.

NOTE that f(x) is neither right continuous nor left continuous at c if f is not defined at c!

f(x) is <u>continuous on the (open) interval (a,b)</u> if f(x) is continuous at every value in the interval (a,b).

f(x) is <u>continuous on the (closed) interval [a,b]</u> if f(x) is:
      1. continuous on the open interval (a,b),
      2. right continuous at a, <u>AND</u>
      3. left continuous at b.

f(x) is said to be simply <u>continuous</u> (without qualification) if f(x) is continuous for all real numbers.

•Example:

Let $f(x) = \begin{cases} x - 1 & x < -3 \\ 2x - 1 & -3 \le x < 0 \\ x^2 - 1 & 0 < x < 2 \\ 5 - x & 2 \le x < 6 \\ -0.99 & x = 6 \\ 2x - 13 & 6 < x \end{cases}$.

Then $f(x)$ is right continuous at -3, because $\lim\limits_{x \to -3^+} f(x) = -7$, and $f(-3) = -7$.

$f(x)$ is also continuous on the open interval $(-3,0)$ and on the <u>half</u>-open interval $[-3,0)$.

Other intervals on which $f(x)$ is continuous are $(-\infty,-3)$, $(0,6)$, and $(6,-\infty)$.

Determining Continuity from a Graph

To decide whether a function is continuous at some value c, we go back to the informal definition of continuity: a function is continuous if we can draw its graph without lifting the pencil off the paper.

Remember that when we talk about continuity <u>at</u> some value c, we are referring to continuity where the <u>x</u>-coordinate is c.

•Example:

Decide whether the function is continuous at -3, 1, and 5.

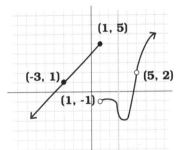

Solution:

The graph goes right through the point (-3,1) without a break. Therefore f(x) is continuous at -3.

The graph jumps from the point (1,5) to the point (1,-1); therefore f(x) is not continuous at 1. Notice, however, that f(x) is left continuous at 1, because $\lim\limits_{x \to -1^-} f(x) = 5$, and f(1) also equals 5.

There is a hole in the graph at (5,2) so f(x) is not continuous at 5.

Limits and Continuity. Exercise 6. Continuity.

For problems 1-11, decide whether the given function is (a) continuous,
(b) left continuous only, (c) right continuous only, or (d) not continuous at x = 2.

1. $f(x) = \begin{cases} 3x & x < 2 \\ 2x + 1.99 & x \geq 2 \end{cases}$

2. $f(x) = \begin{cases} 3x & x < 2 \\ x - 1 & x = 2 \\ 2x + 2 & x \geq 2 \end{cases}$

3. $f(x) = \begin{cases} 3x & x < 2 \\ x - 1 & x = 2 \\ x + 4 & 3 \leq x \end{cases}$

4. $f(x) = \begin{cases} \frac{5x}{x-2} & x < 2 \\ x + 4 & 2 \leq x \end{cases}$

5. $f(x) = \begin{cases} 3x & x < 2 \\ 8 - x & 2 < x \end{cases}$

6. $f(x) = \begin{cases} 3x & x < 2 \\ x^2 + x & x = 2 \\ x + 4 & 2 < x \end{cases}$

7. $f(x) = \begin{cases} 3x & x < 2 \\ x^2 + x & x = 2 \\ x + 5 & 2 < x \end{cases}$

8. $f(x) = \begin{cases} \frac{5x}{x-2} & x < 2 \\ 3x & x = 2 \\ x + 5 & 2 < x \end{cases}$

9. $f(x) = \begin{cases} 3x & x < 2 \\ 8 & x = 2 \\ \frac{5x}{x-2} & 2 < x \end{cases}$

10. $f(x) = \begin{cases} 3x & x < 2 \\ 5x - 4 & x = 2 \\ \frac{5x}{x-2} & 2 < x \end{cases}$

11. $f(x) = \begin{cases} 3x & x < 2 \\ 2x & x = 2 \\ x + 1 & 2 < x \end{cases}$

In problems 12-16, decide whether the graphed function is (a) continuous,
(b) left continuous, (c) right continuous, or (d) not continuous at x = -3.

12.

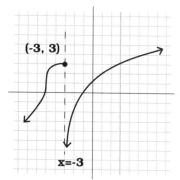

(-3, 3)

x=-3

13.

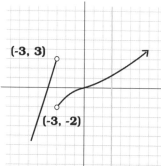

(-3, 3)

(-3, -2)

14.

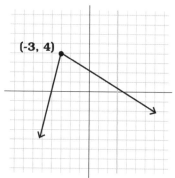

(-3, 4)

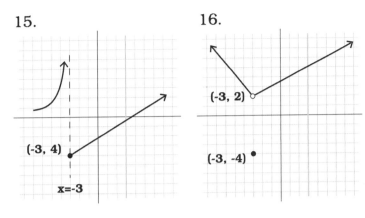

15.

16.

(-3, 4)

x=-3

(-3, 2)

(-3, -4)

For problems 17-20, find the intervals on which the given function is continuous. Always choose the largest possible interval.

17. $f(x) = \begin{cases} 3e^2 & x \le -4 \\ \ln x & 0 < x \end{cases}$

18. $g(x) = \begin{cases} \frac{\sin x}{x+4} & x \le 0 \\ x^2 + x & 0 < x < 3 \\ 2x + 1 & 3 \le x \end{cases}$

19. $h(x) = \begin{cases} \ln(-x) & x < -4 \\ x + 5 & 0 \le x < 3 \\ 17 & x = 3 \\ \sqrt{x + 61} & 3 < x \end{cases}$

20. $f(x) = \begin{cases} \ln(-x) & x < -4 \\ x + 5 & 0 \le x < 3 \\ \sqrt{x + 61} & 3 \le x \end{cases}$

Part 7 Continuity and Limits of Rational Functions

As mentioned in the previous section, rational functions are continuous everywhere except for values of x which cause the denominator to equal zero. Therefore, we can calculate $\lim_{x \to c}$ for a rational function f by using the following procedure. First, substitute x = c into the numerator and the denominator. Then:

1. If we get <u>nonzero</u> values both on the top and on the bottom, then $\lim_{x \to c} f(x)$ is simply f(c).

2. If we get zero on top and a nonzero value on the bottom, then $\lim_{x \to c} f(x) = 0$.

3. If we get zero on the bottom and a nonzero value on top, then $\lim_{x \to c} f(x)$ is undefined.

4. If we get zero on both the top and the bottom, then we can reduce the fraction by cancelling the factor (x-c) from both the top and the bottom (**Straight Forward Pre-Calculus** tells us (truthfully!) that (x-c) must be a factor of both the numerator and the denominator). Then we try again by substituting x = c into the new function.

•Examples:

Find the limits of the following functions as x goes to 3:

a. $\dfrac{x^2-8}{x^2-6x+8}$ b. $\dfrac{x^2-9}{x^2-6x+8}$

c. $\dfrac{x^2-8}{x^2-6x+9}$ d. $\dfrac{x^2-9}{x^2-5x+6}$

Solutions:

a. When we substitute x = 3, the value of the numerator is 1, and the value of the denominator is -1. Therefore, the limit is $\frac{1}{-1}$, or -1.

b. The value of the numerator when x = 3 is 0; the value of the denominator is -1. Therefore, the limit we seek is 0.

c. This time the numerator value is 1 and the denominator value is 0. Therefore, the limit is undefined.

d. Both the numerator and the denominator have a value of zero when x = 3 is substituted. Therefore, (x-3) is a factor of both the numerator and the denominator, as shown:

$$\frac{x^2-9}{x^2-5+6} = \frac{(x-3)(x+3)}{(x-3)(x-2)}$$

When we cancel the factor (x-3) from both the top and bottom, the new function is $\frac{x+3}{x-2}$.

By substituting x = 3 into the new function, we get the value $\frac{6}{1}$, or 6. Therefore $\lim\limits_{x\to 3} \dfrac{x^2-9}{x^2-5x+6} = 6$.

Limits and Continuity. Exercise 7. Continuity and Limits of Rational Functions.

Find each limit:

1. $\lim\limits_{x\to 1} \dfrac{x^2-2x+1}{x^3+3x^2-6x+2}$

2. $\lim\limits_{x\to 1} \dfrac{x^2-2x+2}{x^3+3x^2-6x+5}$

3. $\lim\limits_{x\to 1} \dfrac{x^2-2x-3}{x^3+x^2-5x+3}$

4. $\lim\limits_{x\to 1} \dfrac{x^3-3x^2+3x-1}{x^3-2x^2+x}$

5. $\lim\limits_{x\to -2} \dfrac{x^3+3x^2+3x+2}{x^3+3x^2+x-2}$

6. $\lim\limits_{x\to -2} \dfrac{x^3-12x-16}{x^3+3x^2-4}$

7. $\lim\limits_{x\to -2} \dfrac{x^2+6x+8}{x^2-2x-8}$

8. $\lim\limits_{x\to -2} \dfrac{x^3-12x-16}{x^2-2x-8}$

9. $\lim\limits_{x \to 4} \dfrac{x^2-2x-8}{x^2-7x+11}$

10. $\lim\limits_{x \to 4} \dfrac{x^2-2x-8}{x^3-6x^2+32}$

11. $\lim\limits_{x \to 4} \dfrac{x^3-12x^2+48x-64}{x^3-6x^2+32}$

12. $\lim\limits_{x \to 4} \dfrac{x^3-x^2-10x-8}{x^3-6x^2+32}$

13. $\lim\limits_{x \to -1} \dfrac{x^3+4x^2+5x+2}{x^3-3x^2+3x+1}$

14. $\lim\limits_{x \to -1} \dfrac{x^2+3x+2}{x+1}$

15. $\lim\limits_{x \to -1} \dfrac{x^3+4x^2+5x+2}{x^3-x^2-5x-3}$

16. $\lim\limits_{x \to -1} \dfrac{x^2+5}{x^2+3x+2}$

Part 8   Consequences of Continuity

The Minimum-Maximum Value Theorem

What is the maximum possible value of the function $f(x) = \frac{1}{x}$?

There is no answer, because $\frac{1}{x}$ gets bigger than any number you can name as x gets close to 0. However, if we restrict our attention to (for example) the <u>closed</u> interval [2,5], then it's fairly easy to see that the maximum of $\frac{1}{x}$ is $\frac{1}{2}$, or 0.5.

Our ability to find a maximum value for $\frac{1}{x}$ on the interval [2,3] depended not only upon the fact the interval was closed but also on the fact that $\frac{1}{2}$ is <u>continuous</u> on that interval. If we had chosen the interval [-2,2], we would still have been unable to find a maximum value for $\frac{1}{x}$. This example leads us to a formal theorem call the Minimum-Maximum Value Theorem.

> If f is continuous on the closed interval [a,b], then f assumes both a maximum and a minimum value on the interval [a,b].

As the example shows, this theorem is not as obvious as it seems!
There are many reasons why a function might not assume its maximum or minimum value on some interval. The four following examples show why.

•Examples:

> 1. Let f(x) = 3x - 4. Then f has neither a maximum nor a minimum on the open interval (-1,6). f(-1) = -7, but -1 is not in the open interval (-1,6). f(-0.99) = -6.97, but -6.97 isn't the minimum value of f(x) on (-1,6), because f(-0.999) =-6.997, which is less than -6.97.

23

Similarly, f(6) = 14, but since 6 is not in the interval (-1,6), 14 isn't the maximum value for f in that interval. We can get function values as close to 14 as we want, but there is always another function value even closer to 14!

2. Let g(x) = $\frac{x}{2x-1}$. Then g has no maximum on the half-open interval [0,∞). As x gets big, g(x) will approach the value of 0.5, but will never equal exactly 0.5. On the other hand, g <u>does</u> have a minimum value on the interval [0,∞), namely g(0) = 0. However, the Minimum-Maximum Value Theorem does not guarantee that such a minimum exists; it just happens to exist in this particular case.

3. The function g(x) = $\frac{x}{2x-1}$ from Example 2 is continuous on the closed interval [-3,-1]. Therefore, the Minimum-Maximum Value Theorem guarantees that g(x) has both a minimum and a maximum value on that interval. In fact, f(-3) = $\frac{3}{7}$ is the minimum value, and g(-1) = $\frac{1}{3}$ is the maximum value of g on that interval.

4. The function h(x)= x + 2^3x^2 - 20x + 5 is a polynominal, and therefore continuous everywhere. Consequently, h(x) has a minimum and a maximum value on the closed interval [-5,4]. The Minimum-Maximum Value Theorem however gives us no help in *finding* the minimum or the maximum value. The facts are that the maximum value is h(-3.3333...) = 56.851851..., and the minimum value is h(2) = -19. The tools for finding the maximum and minimum values will be discussed later in the book.

The Intermediate Value Theorem and Its Applications

Suppose you are drawing a graph of a continuous function, and further suppose that f(-6) = 11. That means that the point (-6,11) will be on the graph. Notice particularly that the point (-6,11) is <u>above</u> the x-axis. Now suppose that f(2) = -5. Then the point (2,-5), which is <u>below</u> the x-axis, is also on the graph.

It is obvious that the only way to move your pencil from one side of a line to the other without lifting the pencil off the paper, is to cross the line somewhere. In the case of the graph we are discussing, the line we have to cross is the x-axis. Since we have to draw a continuous graph which goes from the point (-6,11) to the point (2,-5), the graph will have to <u>cross</u> the x-axis somewhere between x = -6 and x = 2.

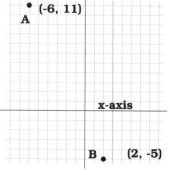

To get from point A to point B, we have to cross the x-axis.

Now, remember that the y-coordinate of any point on the x-axis is zero. Therefore, the value of the function is zero at the point where the graph crosses the x-axis. To put this discussion into mathematical language:

Intermediate Value Theorem

> Let $f(x)$ be continuous on the interval $[a,b]$, and suppose that $f(a)$ and $f(b)$ have opposite signs (i.e., one of them is positive and one is negative). Then there is at least one number c, between a and b, such that $f(c) = 0$. In other words, f has at least one zero between a and b.

•Examples:

> If $f(x) = x^3 + 7x^2 - 2x - 37$, then $f(-6) = 11$, and $f(2) = -5$. Therefore, there is a number c between -6 and 2 such that $f(c) = 0$.
>
> On the other hand, suppose $g(x) = \frac{3}{x}$. Then $g(-1) = -3$, and $g(1) = 3$. However, $g(x)$ is not continuous on the interval $[-1,1]$ so the Intermediate Value Theorem does not assure us that g has a zero between -1 and 1 (and in fact it doesn't).

Approximation of Zeros

Let $f(x) = x^3 + 7x^2 - 2x - 37$. Then $f(-6) = 11$, and $f(2) = -5$. Also f is continuous everywhere because f is a polynomial. Therefore, f has a zero between -6 and 2. Of course, we don't know exactly where that zero is (in fact, there may be more than one), but the Intermediate Value Theorem can help us to get an approximate answer.

The procedure we will use is a simple example of the idea of "successive approximation": We take a guess at the answer, and do some calculations with our guess. The calculations then lead us to a more accurate guess. Then we repeat the procedure with the new guess, and continue repeating until we reach the level of accuracy we require (or until we are just plain tired of the whole thing!). In this case, -2 might be a logical guess, since -2 is half way between -6 and 2. A calculation shows that $f(-2) = -13$. Now we have a <u>new</u> pair of numbers, namely -6 and -2, such that $f(-6)$ and $f(-2)$ have opposite signs ($f(-6)$ is positive, and $f(-2)$ is negative). Therefore f has a zero between -6 and -2.

We have narrowed our search! Originally we knew that f had a zero between -6 and 2 (an interval of length 8), but now we know there is a zero between -6 and -2 (an interval of length 4). So once again, we choose a number in the middle of the interval (-6,-2). This time, let's choose -4. We find that $f(-4) = 19$. Since $f(-4)$ is positive and $f(-2)$ is negative, there is a zero of f between -2 and -4. So at each stage of the game, we choose a number in the interval bounded by the last two x values which gave us opposite signs when substituted into f.

Below we show a table which gives each guess, the sign and value of f when the guess is substituted into f, the resulting interval in which we know is a zero of f, and the new guess:

Old Guess (x)	f(x)	New Interval	Next Guess (new x)
-2	- (-13)	(-6,-2)	-4
-4	+ (19)	(-4,-2)	-3
-3	+ (5)	(-3,-2)	-2.5
-2.5	- (-3.875)	(-3,-2.5)	-2.75
-2.75	+ (0.6406)	(-2.75,-2.5)	-2.625
-2.625	- (-1.6035)	(-2.75,-2.625)	-2.6875
-2.6875	- (-0.4773)	(-2.75,-2.6875)	-2.71875
-2.71875	+ (0.08279)	(-2.71875,-2.6875)	-2.703
-2.703	- (-0.19922)	(-2.71875,-2.703)	-2.711
-2.711	- (-0.0559)	(-2.71875,-2.711)	-2.715
-2.715	+ (0.0157)	(-2.715,-2.711)	-2.713
-2.713	- (-0.0201)	(-2.715,-2.713)	-2.714
-2.714	- (-0.0022)	(-2.715,-2.714)	-2.7145
-2.7145	+ (0.00675)	(-2.7145,-2.714)	-2.7142
-2.7142	+ (0.00138)	(-2.7142,-2.714)	-2.7141

So we see that -2.7141 is within .0001 of an actual zero of f(x). Notice that it is not necessary to choose a number exactly in the middle of the interval for each guess. In the table above, we chose the number in the exact middle of the interval until we got to the interval (-2.71875,-2.6875). Then we started choosing numbers which had a more convenient number of decimal places. [HOWEVER: some books (and some calculus courses) teach a method called the "Bisection Method", which requires that you always choose the number exactly halfway between the lower and upper boundaries of the interval. In any case, each guess must always be chosen from the interval formed by the last two x values which had function values with opposite signs.]

The process above can be tedious, but the traditional approaches to solving equations won't work in this case since f(x) cannot be factored into factors with rational coefficients. Later on, when we have developed the more powerful machinery of calculus, we will discuss a much faster method of successive approximations. That more powerful method could have given us the right answer (-2.714122823) to the nearest billionth, in only four tries!

Limits and Continuity. Exercise 8. Consequences of Continuity.

In problems 1-6, find an approximate solution to the equation, within .01 of the exact answer. Begin with the given interval.

1. $x^3 + 4x^2 + x + 12 = 0$ $(-5,-4)$ 2. $2x^3 + 4x^2 + x + 12 = 0$ $(-3,-2)$

3. $(x-5)^3 + 12 = 0$ $(2,3)$ 4. $e^x + x = 15$ $(2,3)$

5. $x - \ln x = 8$ $(10,11)$ 6. $\frac{\tan x}{x} = 10$ $(1,2)$

For problems 7-12, find an interval of length 1 which contains a zero of the given function. There will always be an answer inside the interval $[-10,10]$.

7. $x^3 + x + 35$ 8. $\ln (x^2 + 2) - 3x$

9. $e^x - 10$ 10. $0.5x^2 - 12x - 50\sin(x+1)$

11. $x^4 - 18x^3 - 6x^2 - x + 5$ 12. $x^3 + x^2 + x + 4$

Derivates

The derivative of a function is another function which measures the rate at which the value of the original function is changing. If the original function is a linear function, then the derivative is simply the slope of the graph of the function (remember that the slope is a measure of the change in y, which is the value of f(x), with respect to the increase in x). For non-linear functions, however, finding the derivative requires more mathematical machinery, including an understanding of limits as covered in the previous chapter. A knowledge of derivatives provides a powerful mathematical tool for solving many kinds of problems.

Part 1 — Slopes and Tangent Lines

Recall that the **slope** of a straight line is a numerical description of the "direction" of the line. Another way of describing the slope is that the slope is the amount by which y will change if x increases by 1.

For convenience, we reprint here some facts and formulas involving the slopes of straight lines:

The slope (m) of a line containing two points (x_1,y_1) and (x_2,y_2) is given by the formula:

$$m = \frac{y_2 - y_1}{x_2 - x_1}.$$

If we solve a linear equation for y, and put the equation in the form
$$y = mx + b$$
then m= the slope of the line, and
b= the y-intercept of the graph—that is, the y-coordinate of the point where the graph crosses the y-axis.

If we are given the slope m of a straight line, and one point (x_1,y_1) which is on that line, then one form of the equation of the line is:
$$y - y_1 = m(x - x_1).$$
(We substitute the given values for x_1, y_1, and m. The x and y in the formula remain x and y.) This is called the point-slope form of the equation of the line.

A positive slope means that the line is going uphill from left to right. In terms of functions, this means that the function is an increasing function.

A negative slope means that the line is going downhill from left to right. In terms of functions, this means that the function is a decreasing function.

A perfectly horizontal line has slope zero.

The slope of a perfectly vertical line is undefined.

Unfortunately, only linear functions have the property that increasing x by 1 causes the same change in y regardless of the original value of x. If f(x) is a non-linear function, then the change in the value of f(x) when x increases by 1 will not necessarily remain constant from one value of x to another.

•Examples:

1. Let y = -4x+9. The equation is in slope-intercept form, so we see that the slope of the graph is -4. Now suppose we choose any value at all for x; let's say 5.

$$\text{If } x = 5, \text{ then } y = (-4)(5)+9$$
$$= -11.$$
Now suppose we increase x by 1, so that x now equals 6.
$$\text{Then:} \quad y = (-4)(6)+9$$
$$= -15.$$

So when we increased x by 1, y decreased by 4. In other words, y changed by -4. If we had begun with x = 1, calculated the value of y, and then repeated the proces s for x = 2, we would have found that y changed from 5 to 1, again a decrease of 4. In fact, we would have decreased y by 4 whenever we increased x by 1, no matter what we chose as our original x value. A slope of -4 means that when we move from any point on the graph to a second point whose x-coordinate is 1 more than the x-coordinate of the first point, the y-coordinate will decrease by 4 regardless of the choice of the starting point.

2. Suppose $f(x) = x^2$.   Then f(1) = 1,
$$f(2) = 4,$$
$$f(3) = 9.$$
Therefore, on the graph of $y = x^2$, an increase in x from 1 to 2 will increase y from 1 to 4, an increase of 3. But an increase in x from 2 to 3 results in an increase of 5 in y (from 4 to 9). So there is no constant slope for the graph of $y = x^2$.

It should not surprise us that the slope cf a non-linear function changes from point to point, since the slope is a measure of the direction of the graph. It is clear that the direction of a non-linear graph is not the same at every point. The graph pictured below is obviously not going in the same direction at point A as it is at point B. However, there should be some way to describe the slope, or direction, of a non-linear graph at a specified point. For example, by "eyeballing" the graph below at point A, we might try to draw a straight line which intersects the graph at point A and which is going in the same direction that the graph is going at that point. That straight line is called the <u>tangent line to the graph of f(x) at the point A.</u> Then we could measure the slope of that line, and call it the slope of the graph itself at point A. The diagram shows an attempt to do exactly that with the slope measured as approximately 2.

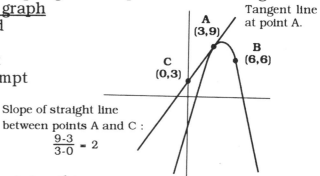

Slope of straight line between points A and C :
$$\frac{9-3}{3-0} = 2$$

It is obviously preferable to have a reliable mathematical method for measuring the slope of a graph at a point rather than having to estimate the tangent line visually and then measuring the slope of that line. And, in fact, there is such a method. We will describe the method informally here, and then make it more precise in the next section.

The difficulty with measuring a slope at just one point of a graph is that the standard slope formula $\left(m = \frac{y_2 - y_1}{x_2 - x_1}\right)$ requires <u>two</u> points. However, there is no law against using two points which are very close together. If we want the slope of the graph of f(x) at point A, we can choose point A as the first of the two points, and some other nearby point on the graph as the second point. Then, if we are lucky, the measured slopes will approach a <u>limit</u> as the second point gets closer and closer to point A.

•Example:

Find the slope at point A of the graph shown above. The graph is of the equation y = f(x) = -x² + 8x - 6, and the point is (3,9).

Solution:

First notice that (3,9) is actually on the graph, because
f(3) = -(3²) + 8 (3) - 6 = 9.

Therefore we will calculate slopes by using (3,9) as the first point, and a series of other points on the of graph y = f(x), whose x-coordinates will get closer and closer to 3. For example, f(3.1) = 9.19. The slope of the straight line between (3,9) and (3.1,9.19) is therefore:
$$\frac{9.19-9}{3.1-3} = 1.9$$

By using other values of x, closer and closer to 3, we will see that the calculated slope approaches 2:

x	f(x)	Slope between (x,f(x))) and (3,9)
3.1	9.19	1.9
3.01	9.0199	1.99
3.001	9.001999	1.999
2.9	8.79	2.1
2.99	8.9799	2.01
2.999	8.997999	2.001

It is important to notice that, in the example above, we used x values both less than <u>and</u> greater than 3 to calculate our slopes. If we hadn't got the same limit for the slope as x approached 3 from above as we did when x approached 3 from below, then the entire result would be invalid and the slope would be undefined.

Once we know the slope of a graph at a given point, we are able to find the equation of the tangent line at that point.

•Example:

Find the equation of the tangent line to the graph of $y = \sqrt{x}$ at the point where x = 0.25

Solution:

We first find the y-coordinate of the point we are interested in, simply by calculating $f(0.25) = \sqrt{0.25} = 0.5$. So our point is (0.25,0.5). We get the other points and the resulting slopes by taking points with x values close to 0.25, similarly to what we did in the previous example:

x	f(x)	Slope between (x,f(x))) and (0.25,0.5)
0.26	0.50990195	0.990195
0.251	0.50099900	0.999002
0.2501	0.50009999	0.999900
0.24	0.48989795	1.010205
0.249	0.49899900	1.001002
0.2499	0.49989999	1.000100

So the limit of the slopes seems to be 1. Using the slope and the point (0.25,0.5), we can use the point-slope formula (given at the beginning of this section) for building the equation of a straight line.

In our case, $y_1 = 0.5$, $m = 1$, and $x_1 = 0.25$. We plug those numbers in and get our final answer:

$$y - 0.5 = 1(x-0.25), \text{ or simplifying, } y = x + 0.25.$$

Derivatives. Exercise 1. Slopes and Tangent Lines.

In problems 1-6, estimate the slope of the graph of $y = f(x)$ at the given point.

1. $f(x) = x^3 - 4x^2 + x - 8$; (2,-14)

2. $f(x) = x^3 + 6x^2 + 12x + 1$; ((-2,-7)

3. $f(x) = |x + 3|$; (-3,0)

4. $f(x) = \sin x$; $(\frac{\pi}{2},1)$

5. $f(x) = e^x$; (ln 5,5)

6. $f(x) = \frac{x+3}{x-1}$; (0,3)

In problems 7-12, find the equation of the tangent line to $y = f(x)$, where x has the given value.

7. $f(x) = x^3 - 4x^2 + x - 8$; $x = 0$

8. $f(x) = x^3 + 6x^2 + 12x + 1$; $x = -1$

9. $f(x) = |x + 3|$; $x = 4$

10. $f(x) = \sin x$; $x = \pi$

11. $f(x) = e^x$; $x = \ln 2$

12. $f(x) = \frac{x+3}{x-1}$; $x = 3$

13. Estimate the slopes of $y = \frac{1}{2}x^2 - 6$ at the x values -2, 0, 2, 5, and 10. Find a pattern in your answers, and use the pattern to speculate about a general rule for the slope of $y = \frac{1}{2}x^2$ at any given point.

14. Estimate the slopes of $y = e^x$ at the x values $\ln(0.5)$, $\ln 3$, $\ln 6$, and $\ln 10$. As in problem 13, try to produce a general rule for finding the slope of $y = e^x$ at any given point.

Part 2 — Definition of a Derivative

In the previous section, we estimated the slope of $y = f(x) = -x^2 + 8x - 6$ at the point (3,9) by calculating the slopes of the straight lines between (3,9) and other points very close to (3,9) on the graph of $y = -x^2 + 8x - 6$. We will now make that procedure more precise by defining the procedure in terms of limits.

•Example:

Find the slope of $y = 3x^2$ at the point (-2,12).

Solution:

We solve the problem by calculating the slope of a straight line connecting (-2,12) and a second point on the graph of $y = 3x^2$. In our calculations, we want to choose a second point which is very close to (-2,12). In fact, what we really want to do is find the limit of the slopes as the second point approaches (-2,12).

The key to our procedure is to define the second point in a clever way. For one thing, if the second point is going to be close to (-2,12), then the x-coordinate of the second point can be described as -2+h, where h is a very small number. Once we have established the x-coordinate as -2+h, the y-coordinate will <u>have</u> to be $3(-2+h)^2$, simply because this second point has to be on the graph of $y = 3x^2$. So, we can calculate the slope of the straight line connecting (-2,12) with $(-2+h, 3(-2+h)^2)$ as:

$$\frac{3(-2+h)^2 - 12}{-2+h-(-2)}, \quad \text{or} \quad \frac{3(-2+h)^2 - 12}{h}.$$

Now, as the second point approaches the first, the value of h will approach zero. The slope we want is the limit of the expression above as h goes to zero.

If we substitute h = 0 into the expression, we will get zero for both the numerator and denominator; so we will have to do some algebraic simplification before we can calculate the limit:

$$\frac{3(-2+h)^2 - 12}{h} = \frac{3(4-4h+h^2)-12}{h} = \frac{12-12h+3h^3-12}{h} = \frac{-12h+3h^2}{h} = \frac{(-12+3h)h}{h} = -12 + 3h$$

Now we can substitute h = 0 into -12 + 3h, and the answer is -12. Therefore, the slope of the graph of $y = 3x^2$ at the point (-2,12) is -12.

As we noted in the last section, non-linear functions have different slopes at different points. The graph of $y = 3x^2$ does not have slope -12 at every point. However, problems 13 and 14 in the previous set of exercises disclosed an interesting fact. In some cases it is possible to devise a <u>formula</u> for computing the slope of the graph of a function at any given value of x. In the case of $f(x) = \frac{1}{2}x^2 - 6$ (Problem 13), the formula is just x itself. In other words, the slope of $y = \frac{1}{2}x^2 - 6$ at any point on the graph is just the x-coordinate of the point. In the case of $y = e^x$ (Problem 14), the slope at any point (x, e^x) is e^x.

In both cases, we can think of the formula for the slope as a function of x: If we want the slope of the graph at a specified point, we take the x-value of the point and substitute it for x in this "slope formula". The formula then calculates the slope of the graph of the original function, at the particular point we are interested in. This new "slope function" is derived from the original function, and for that reason is called the *derivative* of the original function. One notation for the derivative of f(x) is f'(x) (which is read *f prime of x*).

33

1. From Problem 13 in the previous set of exercises, we know that the slope of $y = \frac{1}{2}x^2 - 6$ at the point $(x, \frac{1}{2}x^2-6)$, is x. Therefore the derivative of $\frac{1}{2}x^2 - 6$ is x.

2. From Problem 14 in the previous set of exercises, we know that the slope of $y = e^x$ at the point (x, e^x) is e^x. Therefore the derivative of e^x is e^x. (In other words, e^x is its own derivative.)

If we know the derivative of a function, we can solve problems such as those in the previous section without resorting to the direct calculation of a limit.

•Example:

Given that the derivative of $f(x) = 3x^2$ is 6x, find the equation of the tangent line to $y = 3x^2$ at the point where $x = -1$.

Solution:

To find the equation of the tangent line, we need three numbers: an x-coordinate (x_1), y-coordinate (y_1), and a slope (m). We already have the x-coordinate (-1). We get the y-coordinate by substituting $x = -1$ into the <u>original</u> function, and the slope by substituting $x = -1$ into the <u>derivative</u>. So:
$$y_1 = 3(-1)^2 = 3$$
$$m = 6(-1) = -6.$$

Therefore the equation of the tangent line to $y = 3x^2$ at the point $(-1,3)$ is $y - 3 = -6(x+1)$, or $y = -6x - 3$.

The only mystery about the example above is: Where did the 6x come from? The answer is shown in the example below.

•Example:

Find the general formula for $f'(x)$, when $f(x) = 3x^2$.

Solution:

The procedure is similar to the one used in the first example in this section, when we calculated the slope of $y = 3x^2$ at the point (-2,12). In that example, we sought $f'(-2)$ by taking

$$\lim_{h \to 0} \frac{f(-2+h)-f(-2)}{h} \qquad \text{where } f(x) = 3x^2.$$

The difference this time is that we are looking for a general formula for f'(x), which means we can't substitute a number for x. So the algebra will be more difficult. The procedure of this kind is:

1. Write the formulas for f(x) and f(x+h) separately.

2. Substitute those formulas into the expression $\frac{f(x+h)-f(x)}{h}$.

3. Simplify the expression algebraically so that the h in the denominator cancels out.

4. Take the limit of the resulting expression as h goes to zero.

We show below the work involved in applying the procedure to the present problem:

$$f(x+h) = 3(x+h)^2 = 3(x^2+2xh+h^2) = 3x^2 + 6xh + 3h^2$$

$$f(x) = 3x^2$$

$$\frac{f(x+h)-f(x)}{h} = \frac{3x^2+6xh+3h^2-3x^2}{h} = \frac{6xh+3h^2}{h}$$

$$= \frac{(6x+3h)h}{h} = 6x + 3h.$$

$$\lim_{h \to 0}(6x + 3h) = 6x.$$

The derivative of f(x) = $3x^2$ is 6x.

The previous example can now be used as an illustration of the formal definition of the derivative of any function.

Definition of the Derivative

The derivative of f(x) is $\lim_{h \to 0} \frac{f(x+h)-f(x)}{h}$.
(If that limit does not exist, then the function has no derivative.)

The direct computation of a derivative using the formula above, can often involve some fairly complicated algebra. We give two examples:

•Example:

Find the derivative of $g(x) = \sqrt{x+2}$.

Solution:

$$g(x + h) = \sqrt{x+h+2}$$
$$g(x) = \sqrt{x+2}$$

Therefore :

$$\lim_{h\to 0} \frac{g(x+h)-g(x)}{h} = \lim_{h\to 0} \frac{\sqrt{x+h+2}-\sqrt{x+2}}{h} \cdot$$

In order to proceed further, we <u>rationalize the numerator</u> by using the difference of squares formula $(a-b)(a+b) = a^2 - b^2$.

$$\frac{\sqrt{x+h+2}-\sqrt{x+2}}{h} = \left(\frac{\sqrt{x+h+2}-\sqrt{x+2}}{h}\right)\left(\frac{\sqrt{x+h+2}+\sqrt{x+2}}{\sqrt{x+h+2}+\sqrt{x+2}}\right)$$

$$= \frac{\left(\sqrt{x+h+2}\right)^2 - \left(\sqrt{x+2}\right)^2}{h\left(\sqrt{x+h+2}+\sqrt{x+2}\right)} = \frac{x+h+2-(x+2)}{h\left(\sqrt{x+h+2}+\sqrt{x+2}\right)}$$

$$= \frac{x+h+2-x-2}{h\left(\sqrt{x+h+2}+\sqrt{x+2}\right)} = \frac{h}{h\left(\sqrt{x+h+2}+\sqrt{x+2}\right)}$$

$$= \frac{1}{\sqrt{x+h+2}+\sqrt{x+2}}$$

We now calculate $\lim_{h\to 0} \dfrac{1}{\sqrt{x+h+2}+\sqrt{x+2}}$ by substituting $h = 0$. So we get:

$$\frac{1}{\sqrt{x+0+2}+\sqrt{x+2}} = \frac{1}{\sqrt{x+2}+\sqrt{x+2}} = \frac{1}{2\sqrt{x+2}}$$

The derivative of $g(x) = \sqrt{x + 2}$ is $\dfrac{1}{2\sqrt{x+2}}$.

•Example:

Find the derivative of $k(x) = \dfrac{2}{3x-4}$.

Solution:

$$k(x + h) = \frac{2}{3(x+h)-4} = \frac{2}{3x+3h-4}$$

$$k(x) = \frac{2}{3x-4}$$

So : $\dfrac{k(x+h)-k(x)}{h} = \dfrac{\frac{2}{3x+3h-4}-\frac{2}{3x-4}}{h}$

$$= \frac{\left(\frac{3x-4}{3x-4}\right)\left(\frac{2}{3x+3h-4}\right) - \frac{2}{3x-4}\left(\frac{3x+3h-4}{3x+3h-4}\right)}{h}$$

$$= \frac{\frac{(3x-4)(2)-2(3x+3h-4)}{(3x-4)(3x+3h-4)}}{h}$$

$$= \frac{\frac{6x-8-6x-6h+8}{(3x-4)(3x+3h-4)}}{h} = \frac{\frac{-6h}{(3x-4)(3x+3h-4)}}{h}$$

$$= \frac{-6}{(3x-4)(3x+3h-4)} \cdot$$

$$\lim_{h \to 0} \frac{-6}{(3x-4)(3x+3h-4)} = \frac{-6}{(3x-4)^2} \quad .$$

Therefore, $k'(x) = \dfrac{-6}{(3x-4)^2}$.

Alternate Notation for the Derivative

If we begin with an equation of the form
$$y = (\text{formula for } f(x))$$
then we sometimes denote the derivative of f(x) as $\dfrac{dy}{dx}$. We can think of this as "the difference in y, over the difference in x"—which is more or less what the slope is, so the idea makes sense.

This notation is more cumbersome than f'(x), but is useful for several kinds of problems which we will deal with later.

The $\dfrac{dy}{dx}$ notation is particularly helpful when we are dealing with several variables in the same problem. The $\dfrac{dy}{dx}$ reminds us that we are dealing with the derivative of the function which describes y as a function of x. Of course, if we have an equation such as
$$s = (\text{formula for } g(r))$$
then g'(r) can be denoted $\dfrac{ds}{dr}$.

Also, sometimes we denote the derivative of a function of x by $\dfrac{d}{dx}$ (formula for the function) so that, for example, the derivative of $2x^3 - 5x + 7$ would be expressed $\dfrac{d}{dx}(2x^3 - 5x + 7)$.

Summary:

1. The slope of a non-linear function is not constant; the slope depends on the value of x.

2. The derivative of a function f(x) is another function which gives the slope of f(x) at each value of x. In other words, the slope of the graph of y = f(x) at a particular value of x can be determined by substituting that value into the derivative.

3. The formal definition of the derivative of f(x) is
$$\lim_{h \to 0} \frac{f(x+h)-f(x)}{h} .$$

4. The slope of y = f(x) at the point where x = c can be computed by substituting x = c into the formula above. The slope is therefore
$$\lim_{h \to 0} \frac{f(c+h)-f(c)}{h}$$

Derivatives. Exercise 2. Definition of a Derivative.

In problems 1-8, find $f'(x)$.

1. $f(x) = 5 + 3x$

2. $f(x) = 5 - 2x^2$

3. $f(x) = 5 + 3x - 2x^2$

4. $f(x) = \frac{2}{5+3x}$

5. $f(x) = \frac{2-7x}{5+3x}$

6. $f(x) = (x-1)^3$

7. $f(x) = \sqrt{5+3x}$

8. $f(x) = \sqrt{x^2 - 2}$

In problems 9-12, find $f'(2)$.

9. $3 - 5x^2$

10. $\frac{3}{5x^2}$

11. $(x + 1)^3$

12. $\sqrt{x^2 + 5}$

In problems 13-16, find the slope of the graph of $y = f(x)$ at $x = -3$.

13. $f(x) = x^2 + x + 1$

14. $f(x) = \frac{8}{x-1}$

15. $f(x) = \frac{2x+8}{x-1}$

16. $f(x) = \sqrt{x^2 - 5}$

17. If $m = (2x - 3)^2$, find $\frac{dm}{dx}$.

18. If $q = \frac{3s+1}{s+3}$, find $\frac{dq}{ds}$.

Part 3: Basic Differentiation Formulas

Calculus would not have achieved the wildy enthusiastic popularity it enjoys today if we had to calculate derivatives by using the procedure given in the previous section. Fortunately, there are formulas for finding the derivatives of most of the common types of functions. This section will discuss some of the most basic formulas.

When we calculate the derivative of a function, we are said to be differentiating the function. The formulas we give below are called **differentiation formulas**.

Formula 1:

$$(f + g)'(x) = f'(x) + g'(x).$$
$$(f - g)'(x) = f'(x) - g'(x).$$

This formula states that the derivative of the sum or difference of two functions is the sum or difference of the derivatives of the two separate functions. Therefore, if a function has several terms, we can differentiate the function term by term.

Formula 2:

> The derivative of any constant function (i.e., f(x) = c for some number c) is <u>zero</u>.

This formula is no suprise, because the graph of a constant function is a horizontal line. And, as we know, the slope of any horizontal line is zero.

Formula 3:

> The derivative of f(x) = mx is m.

Again this is no surprise, because the line y = mx has slope m.

Formula 4:

> If k is any number, then $(kf)'(x) = k f'(x)$.

For example, the derivative of 7f(x) is 7 times the derivative of f(x).

Formula 5:

> If $f(x) = ax^n$, then $f'(x) = nax^{n-1}$. This formula applies for any value of n: positive, negative, fractional, or whatever.

•Examples:

> Find the derivatives of:
>
> a. $f(x) = 6$ b. $f(x) = 2x$
>
> c. $f(x) = 2x - 6$ d. $g(x) = 1.7654321(2x - 6)$
>
> e. $h(x) = 3x^2$ f. $r(x) = \frac{3}{x}$
>
> g. $f(x) = \frac{-3}{2x}$ h. $f(x) = \sqrt{x} - 5x^7 + 4$
>
> Solutions:
>
> a. $f(x) = 6$ is a constant, so $f'(x) = 0$ by Formula 2.
> b. $f(x) = 2x$ has the form $f(x) = mx$, so Formula 3 applies, and $f'(x) = 2$.
> c. We already know from (a) and (b) that the derivatives of 2x and 6 are 2 and 0 respectively. Therefore, Formula 1 tells us that the derivative of f(x) = 2x-6 is 2-0, or 2.

d. By using Formula 4, the derivative of g(x) = 1.7654321(2x-6) is 1.7654321 times the derivative of 2x-6. We found in (c) that the derivative of 2x-6 is 2, so the derivative of 1.7654321(2x-6) is 1.7654321(2) = 3.5308642.

e. For h(x) = $3x^2$, Formula 5 applies with n = 2, a = 3, so that the derivative of h(x) = $3x^2$ is $(2)(3)x^1$, or 6x.

f. The function r(x) = $\frac{3}{x}$ can be rewritten as r(x) = $3x^{-1}$. (THIS IS AN IMPORTANT IDEA! When differentiating, we often rewrite functions with exponents instead of fractions or radicals when possible.) Then Formula 5 applies again, r'(x) = $(-1)(3)x^{-2}$. The derivative is -3x, or $\frac{-3}{x^2}$.

g. This works exactly like (f). This time we rewrite f(x) as $\frac{-3}{2}x^{-1}$. That means the derivative will be $(-1)(\frac{-3}{2})x^{-2}$, or $\frac{3}{2x^2}$.

h. We can rewrite f(x) as $x^{\frac{1}{2}}$ - $5x^7$ + 4. We find the derivative by differentiating each term separately and putting it all together. The answer is $\frac{1}{2}x^{-\frac{1}{2}}$ - $35x^6$, or $\frac{1}{2\sqrt{x}}$ - $35x^6$.

•Further Examples:

a. If g(x) = $\frac{4}{3\sqrt{x}}$, find g'(25).

b. Find the slope of the graph y = $6x^7$-$19x^4$-10x+2 at the point (-1,25).

c. Find the equation of the tangent line to y = $\frac{8}{x}$, where x = 2.

Solutions:

a. First we write the function as $\frac{4}{3}x^{-\frac{1}{2}}$. Using Formula 5:
$$g'(x) = -\frac{2}{3}x^{-\frac{3}{2}}. \text{ And, } g'(25) = -\frac{2}{3}(25)^{-\frac{3}{2}} = -\frac{2}{3}\left(\frac{1}{125}\right) = \frac{-2}{375}.$$

b. Because of Formula 1, we can differentiate each term separately and put it all together. The derivative of the "+2" term is zero by Formula 2. The derivative of the "-10x" term is -10, by using Formula 3. We differentiate the other two terms using Formula 5, so that the derivative is $42x^6$+ $76x^3$- 10. We find the slope at (-1,25) by substituting -1 into the derivative. The answer is -44.

c. We rewrite the original equation as y = $8x^{-1}$. Then $\frac{dy}{dx}$=-$8x^{-2}$, or $-\frac{8}{x^2}$. Substituting x = 2 into the derivative, we calculate the slope as -2. By substituting x = 2 into the original function, we get the y-coordinate of the point we are interested in, which is y=4. So we have the values: x_1= 2, y_1= 4, m = -2.

Substituting those values into the formula $y - y_1 = m(x - x_1)$, and then simplifying, we get: $y = -2x + 8$.

•Example:

Define all x values where the graph of an arbitrary quadratic, $y = ax^2 + bx + c$, has a horizontal tangent line.

Solution:

As noted earlier, a horizontal tangent line has slope zero. Consequently, we seek all points where the derivative is equal to zero. The derivative of $ax^2 + bx + c$ is $2ax + b$. So we want to solve the equation: $2ax + b = 0$.

The solution is $x = \frac{-b}{2a}$.

Recall (from **Straight Forward Algebra, Book 2**, Chapter 5) that the graph of the quadratic equation $y = ax^2 + bx + c$ is a parabola, which looks like one of the shapes below. As we can see, the one point on the graph where the tangent line is horizontal is at the vertex (the highest or lowest point on the graph) where the graph turns around. What we have discovered in this example is that the vertex can always be located as the point where $x = \frac{-b}{2a}$.

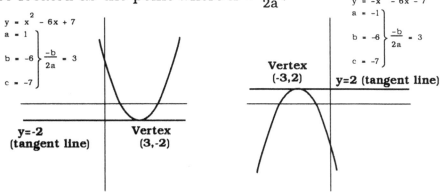

Derivatives. Exercise 3. Basic Differentiation Formulas

In problems 1-4, find $f'(x)$.

1. $f(x) = 5x^4 - 4x^3 + x^2 - 3$ 2. $f(x) = 6 - 5x + \sqrt{x}$

3. $f(x) = 6 - 5x + \sqrt{2x}$ 4. $f(x) = \frac{5}{2\sqrt{x}} - \frac{3}{x^5} + 7x^{\frac{7}{8}} - 12x$

In problems 5-8, find $g'(8)$.

5. $g(x) = 3x^2 - 27x + 5$

6. $g(x) = 3x^2 - 27x^{\frac{2}{3}} + 5$

7. $g(x) = \frac{24}{5x} - 27x^{\frac{2}{3}} + 5$

8. $g(x) = \frac{24}{5x} - 27x^{\frac{2}{3}} + \pi$

In problems 9-12, find the slope of the graph at $x = 4$.

9. $y = x^2 - 7x + 12$

10. $y = x^3 - 7x^2 + 12x - 19$

11. $y = x^3 - 7x^2 + \frac{60}{\sqrt{x}} - 19$

12. $y = 4x^3 - 15x^2 + \frac{1}{2\sqrt{x}} - 9$

In problems 13-16, find $\frac{dx}{dt}$.

13. $x = 4t^5 - 4t^{\frac{1}{5}} + 7$

14. $x = t^3 - t^2 - 5t + 12$

15. $x = \frac{4}{t^5} + 4t^3 - 6t$

16. $x = 5\sqrt{t} - 6t + 12t^3$

In problems 17-20, find the equation of the tangent line at $x = -2$.

17. $y = 5x - 12$

18. $y = 3x - \frac{1}{2}x^2 - 14$

19. $y = x^3 + 3x^2 + 5x - 16$

20. $y = \frac{-12}{x} + x^2 + 6x - 20$

In problems 21-24, find each point (x- and y-coordinates) where the graph has a horizontal tangent.

21. $y = 5x^2 - 60x + 173$

22. $y = x^3 + 4x^2 - 16x - 50$

23. $y = 3x^4 + 8x^3 - 18x^2 + 71$

24. $y = \frac{3}{x^2} + 8$

Part 4 — Product and Quotient Rules

We begin with a....

BIG TIME WARNING

Although a formula in the previous section told us that the derivative of the sum or difference of two functions is the sum or difference of the derivatives of the individual functions, THE SAME IDEA DOES NOT APPLY TO PRODUCTS AND QUOTIENTS. The derivative of the product of two functions is NOT the product of the two derivatives; the derivative of the quotient of two functions is NOT the quotient of the individual derivatives.

•Example:

Let $f(x) = 2x-5$.
$\quad g(x) = x^2$.

Find:

a. The derivative of $fg(x)$.

b. The product of derivatives of $f(x)$ and $g(x)$.

c. The derivative of $\frac{f(x)}{g(x)}$.

d. The quotient of $\frac{f'(x)}{g'(x)}$.

Solution:

a. The product function $fg(x)$ is $(2x-5)(x^2) = 2x^3-5x^2$.

   The derivative is $6x^2-10x$, using the standard formula.

b. Using the standard formulas, $f'(x) = 2$, and $g'(x) = 2x$.

   Therefore, the product of the two derivatives is $4x$.

c. The quotient function $\frac{f(x)}{g(x)}$ is $\frac{2x-5}{x^2} = \frac{2x}{x^2} - \frac{5}{x^2} = 2x^{-1} - 5x^{-2}$.

   Therefore, the derivative is $-2x^{-2} + 10x^{-3}$, or $\frac{-2}{x^2} + \frac{10}{x^3}$.

d. The separate derivatives of f and g, as noted in Part b, are $f'(x) = 2$,

   and $g'(x) = 2x$. So the quotient $\frac{f'(x)}{g'(x)}$ is $\frac{2}{2x} = \frac{1}{x}$.

The moral of this example is that the *answers to Part a and b were different, and the answers to Parts c and d were different*, which verifies the warning given at the beginning of this section. You CANNOT get the derivative of a product or quotient of two functions by taking the product or quotient of the separate derivatives!

Fortunately, there are formulas which tell us how to find the derivatives of products or quotients of two functions, in terms of the separate derivatives of the individual functions. We give those formulas as:

Product and Quotient Formulas

Product Formula: $(fg)' = f'g + g'f$.

Quotient Formula: $(\frac{f}{g})' = \frac{f'g-g'f}{g^2}$.

Note that we have left out the *(x)* after each function, because the formulas are easier to read and memorize that way. There will be some situations in the future, however, in which the *(x)* (or *(t)*, or whatever) will be necessary in order to keep track of what we are doing.

•Example:

a. Let $y = (6-4x)(2x^2-7x+1)$. Find $\frac{dy}{dx}$ by using the product formulas already given.

b. Find $\frac{dy}{dx}$ for the equation in Example a. by multiplying the factors, simplifying, and differentiating term by term.

c. Let $k(x) = \frac{3x^2+1}{2x-1}$. Find $k'(x)$ by using the quotient formula above.

Solutions:

a. An effective, systematic way to use the product and quotient rules is to express the given function as fg or $\frac{f}{g}$, and then write a 2-by-2 matrix:

$$f = 6 - 4x \qquad f' = -4$$
$$g = 2x^2 - 7x + 1 \qquad g' = 4x - 7$$

Then it is easy to substitute the expressions into the formula $f'g + g'f$:

$$\frac{dy}{dx} = (-4)(2x^2 - 7x + 1) + (4x - 7)(6 - 4x)$$
$$= -8x^2 + 28x - 4 + (-16x^2 + 52x - 42)$$
$$= -24x^2 + 80x - 46$$

b. If we multiply the two factors together, we get $-8x^3 + 40x^2 - 46x + 6$. Differentiating term by term, we find that $\frac{dy}{dx} = -24x^2 + 80x - 46$; the same answer that we reached in Part a.

c. We set up another 2-by-2 matrix for $\frac{f}{g}$:

$$f = 3x^2 + 1 \qquad f' = 6x$$
$$g = 2x - 1 \qquad g' = 2$$

Substituting into the formula $\frac{f'g-g'f}{g^2}$, we find:

$$k'(x) = \frac{6x(2x-1)-2(3x^2+1)}{(2x-1)^2}$$
$$= \frac{12x^2-6x-6x^2-2}{(2x-1)^2} = \frac{6x^2-6x-2}{(2x-1)^2}$$

We can now solve the same kinds of problems we solved in the previous section, except that we have a larger collection of functions which we know how to differentiate.

•Examples:

a. Find $f'(4)$ if $f(x) = (2x^2\text{-}3x+4)(\text{-}5x^2+6\sqrt{x} - \frac{8}{x})$.

b. Find the equation of the tangent line to $y = \frac{2x+3}{3x-2}$, where $x = 5$.

c. Find all points where the tangent line to $y = \frac{2x+3}{3x-2}$ is horizontal.

Solutions:

a. We could, of course, multiply the two factors together and then differentiate, but that would be messy. Expressing our function as $f_1 g_1$ (we use the "1" subscript to distinguish f_1 from the original f), we build our 2-by-2 matrix:

$$f_1 = 2x^2 - 3x + 4 \qquad\qquad f_1' = 4x - 3$$
$$g_1 = -5x^2 + 6x^{\frac{1}{2}} - 8x^{-1} \quad g_1' = -10x + 3x^{-\frac{1}{2}} + 8x^{-2}$$

(rewriting terms in exponential form)

By the product rule,

$$f'(x) = (4x - 3)(-5x^2 + 6x^{\frac{1}{2}} - 8x^{-1}) + (-10x + 3x^{-\frac{1}{2}} + 8x^{-2})(2x^2 - 3x + 4).$$

At this point, it is probably easier to substitute $x = 4$ than it is to multiply and collect like terms algebraically. We have
$f'(4) = (13)(-70)+(24)(-38) = -1822$.

b. We use the quotient rule to find the derivative of $\frac{f}{g}$, where:

$$f = 2x+3 \qquad\qquad f_1' = 2$$
$$g = 3x-2 \qquad\qquad g_1' = 3$$

So, $\frac{f'g+g'f}{g^2}$ is $\frac{-13}{(3x-2)^2}$. Substituting $x = 5$, we find that the slope of the tangent line is $\frac{-1}{13}$. By substituting $x = 5$ into the original function, we find that the y-coordinate of the point we want is equal to $\frac{13}{13}$ or 1. The point-slope formula then gives $y = -\frac{1}{13}x + \frac{18}{13}$ as the equation of the tangent line.

c. As we discovered in Part b, the derivative of the function is $\frac{-13}{(3x-2)^2}$. Since a horizontal tangent line has slope equal to zero, we solve the equation $-\dfrac{13}{(x-2)^2} = 0$. We immediately see that there are no solutions, because A FRACTION IS EQUAL TO ZERO ONLY WHEN THE NUMERATOR IS EQUAL TO ZERO. The numerator in this case is -13, which cannot be equal to zero no matter what x is.

Some functions are complicated enough that we must use both the quotient rule and the product rule, or the product rule more than once, to differentiate them.

•Examples:

Find the derivatives of:

a. $f(x) = \dfrac{2x-3}{(3x-4)(4x-5)}$

b. $f(x) = \left(\dfrac{x-3}{3x+2}\right)\left(\dfrac{2x^2+3x+9}{x^2-8x}\right)$

c. $f(x) = (2x - 3)(3x - 4)(4x - 5)$

Solutions:

a. We could, of course, multiply the denominator out and then use the quotient rule in the standard way, but we will leave the denominator factored to illustrate the procedure to be used when we need both the product and the quotient rule in the same problem. The first step in problems of this kind is to <u>identify the basic form of the function</u>. In this problem, the basic form is a <u>quotient</u>, not a product. The function, as written, can be expressed as $\frac{f}{g}$. It cannot be written as a product fg unless we rewrite it in a different form. So we set up a 2-by-2 matrix:

$$f_1 = 2x-3 \qquad\qquad f_1' = 2$$
$$g_1 = (3x-4)(4x-5) \qquad g_1' = \boxed{}$$

We leave an empty box for g_1', because we will need to use the product rule to get the derivative of g_1. We can express g_1 as $f_2 g_2$, where:

$$f_2 = 3x-4 \qquad\qquad f_2' = 3$$
$$g_2 = 4x-5 \qquad\qquad g_2' = 4$$

Substituting into the product rule $f_2' g_2 + g_2' f_2$,we get:

3(4x - 5) + 4(3x - 4), or

24x - 31.

So we put 24x - 31 into the empty box for g_1' in our first matrix setup above. That now looks like this:

$$f_1 = 2x-3 \qquad\qquad f_1' = 2$$
$$g_1 = (3x-4)(4x-5) \qquad g_1' = \boxed{24x-31} \ .$$

We now substitute these expressions into the quotient formula, $\dfrac{f_1' g_1 - g_1' f_1}{g^2}$, because the original function is a quotient. The final answer is then $\dfrac{-24x^2+72x-53}{(3x-4)^2(4x-5)^2}$.

b. The basic form of this function is a product, $f_1 g_1$, where:

$$f_1 = \frac{x-3}{3x+2} \qquad\qquad\qquad f_1' = \boxed{}$$

$$g_1 = \frac{2x^2+3x+9}{x^2-8x} \qquad\qquad g_1' = \boxed{}$$

We fill in the empty boxes by writing f_1 as $\dfrac{f_2}{g_2}$, where:

$$f_2 = x-3 \qquad\qquad f_2' = 1$$
$$g_2 = 3x+2 \qquad\qquad g_2' = 3$$

So that the value of f_1' in the first matrix above is $\dfrac{f_2' g_2 - g_2' f_2}{g_2^2}$, or $\dfrac{11}{(3x+2)^2}$.

To fill the empty box for g_1', we express g_1 as $\dfrac{f_3}{g_3}$, where:

$$f_3 = 2x^2+3x+9 \qquad\qquad f_3' = 4x+3$$
$$g_3 = x^2-8x \qquad\qquad\quad g_3' = 2x-8$$

Now we get the value of g_1' in our original setup by using the quotient formula $\dfrac{f_3' g_3 - g_3' f_3}{g_3^2}$: $g_1' = \dfrac{-19x^2-18x+72}{(x^2-8x)^2}$ (after simplification). Now our original 2-by-2 set up looks like this:

$$f_1 = \frac{x-3}{3x+2} \qquad\qquad f_1' = \boxed{\frac{11}{(3x+2)^2}}$$

$$g_1 = \frac{2x^2+3x+9}{x^2-8x} \qquad g_1' = \boxed{\frac{-19x^2-18x+72}{(x^2-8x)^2}}$$

Since this is a product, we use the formula $f_1' g_1 + g_1' f_1$, which gives us a final answer, after algebraic simplification, of:

$$\frac{11(2x^2+3x+9)}{(3x+2)^2(x^2-8x)} + \frac{(x-3)(-19x^2-18x+72)}{(3x+2)(x^2-8x)^2}$$

or

$$\frac{-35x^4-64x^3+291x^2-1188x-432}{(3x+2)^2(x^2-8x)^2}$$

c. This function is a product of three factors. But the product formula for differentiation applies only to products of two factors. So we have to express the original function as a product of only two factors. We express our original function now as $f_1 g_1$, where:

$$f_1 = 2x-3 \qquad\qquad f_1' = 2$$
$$g_1 = (3x-4)(4x-5) \qquad\qquad g_1' = \boxed{}$$

Since g_1 is a product of two functions, we use the product formula to find g_1. Here is the setup:

$$g_1 = f_2 g_2, \text{ where:}$$

$$f_2 = 3x-4 \qquad\qquad f_2' = 3$$
$$g_2 = 4x-5 \qquad\qquad g_3' = 4$$

Therefore g_1' above is equal to $3(4x-5) + 4(3x-4) = 24x - 31$.

Now our original setup is:

$$f_1 = 2x-3 \qquad\qquad f_1' = 2$$
$$g_1 = (3x-4)(4x-5) \qquad\qquad g_1' = \boxed{24x-31}$$

Substituting into the product formula $f_1'g_1 + g_1'f_1$, we get, after simplification,

$$72x^2 - 196x + 133.$$

Derivatives. Exercise 4. Product and Quotient Rules.

In problems 1-4 find $f'(x)$. Leave the answer factored when using the product rule. When using the quotient rule, simplify the numerator only.

1. $f(x) = (3x^2 - 4x - 6)(\frac{3}{5\sqrt{x}} - 2x^7 + 2x)$

2. $f(x) = \frac{4x-3}{7-6x}$

3. $f(x) = (1 - 2x + 3x^2)(-4x^3 + 5x^4 - 6x^5)$

4. $f(x) = \frac{4x^3-5x^4+6x^5}{2x+1}$

In problems 5-8, find $f'(9)$.

5. $f(x) = (x^{\frac{3}{2}} + 5x - 2)(\frac{36}{x} + 4x^2)$

6. $f(x) = \frac{2x - \sqrt{x}}{29 - 3x}$

7. $f(x) = \frac{2x^2 - 15x - 20}{6x - 3\sqrt{x} - 7}$

8. $f(x) = \left(\frac{x+7}{x-1}\right)\left(\frac{2x}{3} + x^2\right)$

In problems 9-12, find the slope of the tangent line where $x = 1$.

9. $y = \frac{2x+1}{x-2}$

10. $y = (2x + 1)(x - 2)(7x^4 - 6x^3 + 5x^2)$

11. $y = (2\sqrt{x} - \frac{3}{x^2})(5 - 7x + 9x^2)$

12. $y = \frac{5 - 7x + 9x^2}{4 - 5x}$

In problems 13-16, find the equation of the tangent line at $x = 0$.

13. $y = \frac{5x+8}{x-2}$

14. $y = (\frac{2}{x^2+1})(3\sqrt{x} + 4x^2 - 2)$

15. $y = (x^2 + 2)(2x - 3)(x^2 - 5)(4 - 3x)$

16. $y = \frac{3x - 4x^5 + 7x^2 - 2}{4x+1}$

In problems 17-18, find all points (x- and y-coordinates) where the tangent line is horizontal.

17. $y = \frac{4x-1}{4x+1}$

18. $y = \frac{3-x}{x^2-8}$

Part 5 · Second, Third, and Nth Derivatives

Since the derivative of a function is another function, the derivative itself (usually) has a derivative of its own. The derivative of the derivative is called the <u>second derivative</u> of the original function. The second derivative is given the notation $f''(x)$. If we begin with an equation: $y =$ (formula for $f(x)$), then the second derivative is also called $\frac{d^2y}{dx^2}$.

Naturally, the process of differentiation can be repeated as many times as we wish, giving third, fourth, fifth, and thirteen-hundred-twenty-seventh derivatives. When the number gets beyond three, the "prime" notation changes to $f^{(n)}(x)$, where "n" stands for the order of the derivative.

•Examples:

a. Find the derivatives of <u>all</u> orders of $f(x) = 3x^3 + 2x^2 - 4x + 5$.

b. If $y = \frac{4x^2 - 5x + 1}{6 - 7x}$, find $\frac{d^2y}{dx^2}$.

c. Find $f''(x)$ when $f(x) = (2x^3 - 5x + 7)(3x^3 - 4x^2 + x)$.

49

Solutions:

a. Using the standard formulas:

$$f'(x) = 9x^2 + 4x - 4$$
$$f''(x) = 18x + 4$$
$$f'''(x) = 18$$
$$f^{(n)}(x) = 0 \text{ for all } n \text{ greater than 3.}$$

b. By using the quotient formula for $\frac{f}{g}$ with $f = 4x^2 - 5x + 1$, and $g = 6 - 7x$, we find the first derivative, which is:

$$\frac{(8x-5)(6-7x)-(-7)(4x^2-5x+1)}{(6-7x)^2}$$

In order to use the quotient formula again, we need to multiply out and collect terms in both the numerator and denominator of the first derivative, which gives us:

$$\frac{-28x^2+48x-23}{49x^2-84x+36}$$

Now we apply the quotient formula again, and after some ghastly calculations, we end up with:

$$\frac{-34}{(6-7x)^3}$$

c. To get the first derivative, we use the product formula as shown:

$$f = 2x^3-5x+7 \qquad\qquad f' = 6x^2-5$$
$$g = 3x^3-4x^2+x \qquad\qquad g' = 9x^2-8x+1$$

Therefore the first derivative is:

$$(6x^2-5)(3x^3-4x^2+x) + (9x^2-8x+1)(2x^3-5x+7)$$

Rather than multiply this out, we will use the product formula twice, once for each of the two products in the first derivative. This procedure gives us:

$$12x(3x^3-4x^2+x) + (9x^2-8x+1)(6x^2-5)$$

for the first product, and

$$(6x^2-5)(9x^2-8x+1) + (18x-8)(2x^3-5x+7)$$

for the second. We note that we have two duplicate expressions when we put the whole thing together, so we get finally:

$$2(6x^2-5)(9x^2-8x+1) + (2x^3-5x+7)(18x-8) + 12x(3x^3-4x^2+x).$$

Derivatives. Exercise 5. Second, Third, and Nth Derivatives.

1. Find the first, second, and third derivatives of f(x) = 3x + 12.

2. Find the first four derivatives of g(x) = 3x^2 + 2x + 12.

3. Find the first seven derivatives of 3x^5 - 2x^2 + 2x + 12.

4. From problems 1-3, formulate a rule which relates p$^{(n)}$(x) to the degree of a polynomial function p(x).

5. Find $\frac{d^2y}{dx^2}$ if y = $\frac{4-7x}{2x+5}$.

6. Find h$^{(3)}$(-4), if h = t^4 - 2t^3 + 3t^2 - 4t + 5.

7. Let f(x) = $\frac{x^2}{2x-3}$. At what points (x- and y-coordinates) does the graph of the derivative f'(x) have a horizontal tangent line?

8. Recall (from Exercise 1, Problem 14 in this chapter (page 32), and the discussion in this section) that the derivative of e^x is e^x. What is f$^{(18)}$(x) if f(x) = e^x?

Part 6 | **Introductory Interpretation of Derivatives**

Finding derivatives is even <u>more</u> fun if we have an idea of what the derivatives mean, and what they are good for. Derivatives actually have many interpretations and many uses, but in this section we will mention only a few applications. We will discuss many other applications, and in greater depth, in Chapter 3.

Recall that for linear equations, a positive slope means the graph is going uphill from left to right, which means the function is increasing. Conversely, a negative slope means that the graph is going downhill from left to right, and that the function is decreasing.

The graphs of non-linear functions do not, in general, go continuously uphill (or conversely, downhill) from left to right throughout their domains. However, the same principle holds for non-linear functions as for linear functions:

Positive slope = uphill from left to right = increasing function.
Negative slope = downhill from left to right = decreasing function.

•Example:

Determine all intervals on which the graph of $y = x^3 - 48x$ is increasing or decreasing.

Solution:

This problem is equivalent to finding out the intervals on which the slope, or derivative, of $x^3 - 48x$ is positive and negative. In other words, the intervals on which $x^3 - 48x$ is increasing will be the solution to the inequality:
$$\frac{d}{dx}(x^3 - 48x) > 0.$$

Similarly, the intervals on which $x^3 - 48x$ is decreasing will be the solution to the inequality:
$$\frac{d}{dx}(x^3 - 48x) < 0.$$

We differentiate $x^3 - 48x$ by the usual procedure, and we get $3x^2 - 48$, or $3(x^2 - 16)$, which factors easily into $3(x - 4)(x + 4)$. We now use the procedure given in **Straight Forward Pre-Calculus**, which calls for us to divide the real number line into intervals based on the zeros of our function (which in this case is the derivative of the original function). The zeros in this case are -4 and 4, so we look at the three intervals shown on the number line below:

By testing one x value from each of the intervals $(-\infty, -4)$, $(-4, 4)$, and $(4, \infty)$, we find that $3x^2 - 48$ is positive on the intervals $(-\infty, -4)$ and $(4, \infty)$, and negative on the interval $(-4, 4)$. Therefore, the original function $x^3 - 48x$ is increasing on the intervals $(-\infty, -4)$ and $(4, \infty)$, and decreasing on the interval $(-4, 4)$.

The simple information about the function $x^3 - 48x$ which we learned in the example above can even give us a <u>very rough</u> idea of what the graph of $y = x^3 - 48x$ looks like. The graph must be going uphill as we go from $-\infty$ to $x = -4$; then it must turn downhill as we go from $x = -4$ to $x = 4$; then it must turn around again, going uphill as x goes to ∞. At this moment, we don't know exactly where those "turnaround" points are, because we don't know the y-coordinates of those points. But we can get those y-coordinates simply by substituting $x = -4$ and $x = 4$ into the <u>original</u> function:

When $x = -4$, $y = (-4)^3 - 48(-4) = 128$.

When $x = 4$, $y = (4)^3 - 48(-4) = -128$.

So a (once again, very rough) graph of $y = x^3 - 48x$ could look like this:

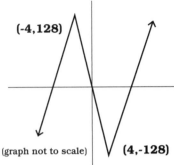

(-4,128)

Of course, we know this is a poor graph because the graph of a non-linear polynomial does not consist of straight lines—it's curved everywhere. But the graph is a useful approximation.

(graph not to scale)   (4,-128)

One of the consequences of the "uphill-downhill" definition of the derivative is that the derivative can tell us where a function reaches its potential maximum value. That's because the graph of a continuous function reaches the "top of a hill" at the point where it stops going upward and turns around to go down. Similarly, if the graph is going downhill, then turns around and starts up, the turnaround point is at the bottom of a valley:

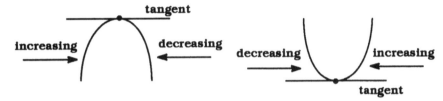

As shown in the diagrams above, the function reaches a potential maximum or minimum wherever the derivative of the function changes sign from + to - or from - to +. If the function and its derivative are continuous, that means those maximum and minimum points occur at values of x for which the derivative is zero—i.e., those points at which the graph has a horizontal tangent line.

BIG TIME WARNING

The points where the graph has a horizontal tangent line are only *potential* maximum and minimum points. We don't know for sure that they represent the maximum or minimum possible value for the function over its entire domain. In this example, point A has a horizontal tangent. But there are obviously points on the overall graph which are higher than A, and other points which are lower than A.

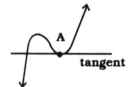

•Example:

Find all potential maximum and minimum points of the function $g(x) = x^3 - 48x$.

53

Solution:

As we saw in the previous example, this function increases as x goes from -∞ to -4, decreases from -4 to 4, and increases again from 4 to ∞. Since the maximum occurs at a point where the function stops increasing and starts decreasing, the point (-4, 128) is a potential maximum point for g(x). Similarly, (4, -128) is a potential minimum point for g(x), since that is where g(x) stops deceasing and begins to increase.

Graphical Interpretation of the Second Derivative

As we know, the second derivative is the derivative of the first derivative. Therefore, a positive second derivative indicates that the first derivative is increasing. Two graphs in which the first derivative is increasing are :

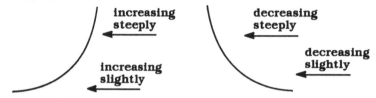

In the first graph, we can see that the slope is always positive, but the slope is increasing because the graph is heading upwards more steeeply at the right than at the left. The second graph shows a more subtle situation: The slope is negative throughout, but the slope at the left end is a <u>large</u> negative number because the graph is going down steeply. At the right end, the graph has flattened out a great deal. The slope is still negative, but is a much smaller negative number—perhaps even close to zero. If the slope has gone from a large negative number to a number close to zero, that means the slope has <u>increased</u>.

Graphs shaped like the two above are called <u>concave up</u>. One way of thinking of the phrase "concave up" is that if the shape is that of a bowl, and it's raining outside, the rain will fall into the inside of the bowl. Another, more technical definition, is that the graph is concave up if the straight line connecting any two points on the graph lies <u>above</u> the graph itself.

The conclusion we reach from the above discussion is:

The graph of a function is concave up on those intervals for which the <u>second derivative</u> is positive. Conversely, the graph is concave down on the intervals for which the second derivative is negative.

Below we show two examples of curves which are concave down. Note that a straight line connecting two points on either of these curves would fall below the curve itself.

•Example:

Characterize the entire length of the graph of
$$y = x^3 + 3x^2 - 45x - 50$$
in terms of increasing, decreasing, and concavity.

Solution:

The first derivative is $3x^2 + 6x - 45$, or $3(x - 3)(x + 5)$. Therefore we determine the sign of the first derivative by looking at the intervals whose endpoints are plus and minus infinity, along with the zeros of $3(x - 3)(x + 5)$, which are -5 and 3. So the intervals to look at are $(-\infty, -5)$, $(-5, 3)$, and $(3, \infty)$. By choosing one value from each of these intervals and substituting the value into the derivative, we find that the derivative is positive when x is in the intervals $(-\infty, -5)$ and $(3, \infty)$. The derivative is negative in the interval $(-5, 3)$. Therefore, the original function is increasing on $(-\infty, -5)$ and $(3, \infty)$, and decreasing on $(-5, 3)$.

The second derivative is $6x + 6$. This expression is zero at $x = -1$, so we look at the intervals $(-\infty, -1)$ and $(-1, \infty)$. We see that $6x + 6$ is negative on $(-\infty, -1)$ and positive on $(-1, \infty)$. So the original function is concave down on the interval $(-\infty, -1)$ and concave on $(-1, \infty)$.

Putting our results on two number lines, we get:

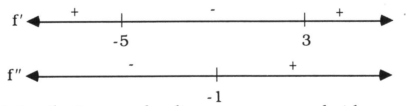

Combining the two number lines, we can see what happens to the function along its entire domain:

Our conclusions are:

On the interval (-∞, -5), the graph of the original function is increasing and concave down, with a shape like this:

On the interval (-5, -1), the graph is decreasing and concave down, which means its shape is like this:

On (-1, 3), the graph is decreasing and concave up, and looks like this:

On (3, ∞), the graph is increasing and concave up, and so looks like this:

Summary:

If the point (c,f(c)) is at the top of a hill or the bottom of a valley on the graph of f(x), then the graph has a horizontal tangent at the point, and f'(c) = 0.

The value of the first derivative of f(x) determines whether f(x) is increasing or decreasing.

The value of the second derivative of f(x) determines the concavity of f(x).

The following three statements are equivalent (that is, they all mean exactly the same thing—if one of them is true, then they're all true):
     1. The graph of f(x) is concave up at x = c.
     2. f'(x) is increasing at x = c.
     3. f''(c) is positive.

The following three statements are equivalent:
     1. The graph of f(x) is concave down at x = c.
     2. f'(x) is decreasing at x = c.
     3. f''(c) is negative.

The following two statements are equivalent:
     1. The graph of f(x) is increasing at x = c.
     2. f'(c) is positive.

The following two statements are equivalent:
     1. The graph of f(x) is decreasing at x = c.
     2. f'(c) is negative.

Derivatives. Exercise 6. Introductory Intrepretation of Derivatives.

For problems 1-6, choose one of the following shapes for the graph of
$y = f(x)$ near $x = -2$:

a.   ⌒   b.   ⌣   c.   ⌐/

d.   ⌊   e.   ⌐   f.   ⌐\

1. $f(x) = 2x^3 + 27x^2 + 84x$ 2. $f(x) = x^3 + 9x^2 + 15x + 2$

3. $f(x) = -x^3 - 12x^2 - 66x - 92$ 4. $f(x) = \frac{x^2+6}{2x-1}$

5. $f(x) = \frac{1}{3}x^3 + 4x^2 + 16x + \frac{56}{3}$ 6. $f(x) = \frac{x+2}{x+4}$

7. Near what point on the graph of $y = \frac{1}{3}x^3 - 8x$ does the graph look like
this ?

    a. $(-6,-24)$ b. $(-2,\frac{40}{3})$ c. $(2,-\frac{40}{3})$ d. $(-2,0)$

8. Near what point on the graph of $y = \frac{1}{3}x^3 + x^2 - 8x$ does the graph
look like this ?

    a. $(-3,24)$ b. $(6,60)$ c. $(-7,-11)$ d. $(-6,12)$

9. Near what point on the graph of $y = x^3 + 3x^2 - 45x + 40$ does the graph
look like this ⌊ ?

    a. $(0,-10)$ b. $(6,14)$ c. $(0,40)$ d. $(-3,95)$

10. Near what point on the graph of $y = \frac{8}{x^2-8x}$ does the graph
look like this ⌐/ ?

    a. $(-1,\frac{8}{9})$ b. $(1,-\frac{8}{7})$ c. $(9,\frac{8}{9})$ d. $(-1,0)$

11. Near what point on the graph of $y = -11x^3 - 33x^2 + 495x + 389$ does the graph look like this $\smallsmile$?

    a. (3,-1280)   b. (-5,-1536)   c. (3,1280)   d. (-1,-128)

12. Near what point on the graph of $y = -11x^3 - 33x^2 + 495x + 389$ does the graph look like this $\frown$?

    a. (3,-1280)   b. (-5,-1536)   c. (3,1280)   d. (-1,-128)

In problems 13-16, divide the domain of the function into intervals based on the signs of the first and second derivatives, and characterize the function in each interval in terms of increasing/decreasing and concavity (similar to the last example in this section).

13. $f(x) = 2x^3 + 6x^2 - 18x - 22$ 14. $g(x) = -x^3 + 6x^2 - 9x - 2$

15. $f(x) = 3x^4 - 16x^3 - 72x^2 + 750$ 16. $k(x) = \frac{1+x^2}{1-x^2}$

Part 7   Trigonometric Limits and Derivatives

Trigonometric functions have all the same rights and privileges as other functions. In particular, trigonometric functions have limits and derivatives.

We begin with two limits whose proofs are based on geometric arguments which can be found in most standard calculus texbooks.

$$\lim_{x \to 0} \frac{\sin x}{x} = 1.$$

$$\lim_{x \to 0} \frac{1-\cos x}{x} = 0.$$

Note that the first limit also implies that $\lim_{x \to 0} \frac{x}{\sin x} = 1$, and the second limit implies that $\lim_{x \to 0} \frac{\cos x - 1}{x} = 0$.

From the two limits above, we can find the derivatives of sin x and cos x.

•Example:

Find the derivative of f(x) = sin x.

58

Solution:

We use the standard limit definition of the derivative,

$$f'(x) = \lim_{h \to 0} \frac{f(x+h)-f(x)}{h}$$

along with the formula for the sine of the sum of two angles:

$$\sin(x + y) = \sin x \cos y + \sin y \cos x.$$

So :

$$f(x + h) = \sin(x + h) = \sin x \cos h + \sin h \cos x$$

$$f(x) = \sin x$$

$$\frac{f(x+h)-f(x)}{h} = \frac{\sin x \cos h + \sin h \cos x - \sin x}{h}$$

$$= \frac{\sin x(\cos h - 1) + \cos x \sin h}{h} = \sin x\left(\frac{\cos h - 1}{h}\right) + \cos x\left(\frac{\sin h}{h}\right)$$

Therefore, $\lim_{h \to 0} \frac{f(x+h)-f(x)}{h} = \lim_{h \to 0} \sin x\left(\frac{\cos h - 1}{h}\right) + \lim_{h \to 0} \cos x\left(\frac{\sin h}{h}\right)$

$$= (\sin x)(0) + (\cos x)(1) = \cos x.$$

So, $\frac{d}{dx}(\sin x) = \cos x.$

A very similar process shows that:

$$\frac{d}{dx}(\cos x) = -\sin x.$$

•Example:

Using the identity $\tan x = \frac{\sin x}{\cos x}$, find the derivative of tan x.

Solution:

We use the quotient rule for $\frac{f_1}{g_1}$, where:

$$f_1 = \sin x \qquad f_1' = \cos x$$
$$g_1 = \cos x \qquad g_1' = -\sin x$$

Substituting these into the formula $\dfrac{g_1 f_1' - g_1' f_1}{g_1^2}$.

we get: $\dfrac{\cos x \cos x + \sin x \sin x}{\cos^2 x} = \dfrac{\cos^2 x + \sin^2 x}{\cos^2 x}$

$$= \dfrac{1}{\cos^2 x} = \sec^2 x.$$

Therefore, the derivative of tan x is $\sec^2 x$.

BIG TIME WARNING

All limits, formulas, and derivatives in calculus which involve trigonometic functions are true only when the number x is measured in <u>radians</u>. Any problems in which angles are given in degrees must first be converted to radians before using the limits or derivatives in this section.

Summary

The derivatives of three primary trigonometric functions are:

$$\dfrac{d}{dx}(\sin x) = \cos x$$

$$\dfrac{d}{dx}(\cos x) = -\sin x$$

$$\dfrac{d}{dx}(\tan x) = \sec^2 x$$

Derivatives. Exercise 7. Trigonometric Limits and Derivatives.

1. Find $f'(x)$ if $f(x) = \sec x$, using the quotient rule and the fact that $\sec x = \dfrac{1}{\cos x}$.

2. Find $g'(x)$ if $g(x) = \csc x$, using the quotient rule and the fact that $\csc x = \dfrac{1}{\sin x}$.

3. Find $\dfrac{d}{dx}(\cot x)$, using $\cot x = \dfrac{1}{\tan x}$.

4. Find out where the graph of sin x has a horizontal tangent in the interval $-2\pi < x < 2\pi$. Compare your answer to what you already know about the graph of sin x.

5. Find all intervals on which cos x is increasing, for $-2\pi < x < 2\pi$, and compare your answer with what you already know about the graph of cos x.

6. Let $g(x) = (3x^2-4x)(\sin x)$, and find $g'(x)$.

7. Let $f(x) = \frac{4\tan x}{5x-7x^3}$, and find $f'(x)$.

8. Identify all points (x- and y-coordinates), with $0 \le x \le 3\pi$, where the graph of $y = x + \cos x$ has a horizontal tangent.

<table>
<tr><td>Part
8</td><td>The Chain Rule</td></tr>
</table>

There are still many comparatively simple functions which we have no easy method of differentiating. For example, so far the only way we can get the derivative of $(3x - 2)^9$ is the impractical method of multiplying the entire expression out and differentiating term by term. Fortunately, there is a differentiation rule which makes such functions much easier to handle.

Chain Rule

> Suppose a given function = f(g) (the composition of the two functions f and g). Then:
> $$(f(g))' = (g') \cdot (f'(g)).$$
>
> The derivative of f(g) is the composition of f' with g, multiplied by g'.

•Example:

> Find the derivative of $(3x - 2)^9$.
>
> Solution:
>
> The function is the composition f(g), where $f(x) = x^9$, and $g(x) = 3x - 2$. Now we use the same 2-by-2 matrix set-up which we introduced for the product and quotient rules:
>
> $\quad\quad f = x^9 \quad\quad\quad\quad\quad f' = 9x^8$
> $\quad\quad g = 3x - 2 \quad\quad\quad\quad g' = 3$
>
> The composition f'(g) is $9(3x-2)^8$. When we multiply that expression by g' as called for in the Chain Rule formula, the answer is $27(3x-2)^8$.
>
> If the reader finds this example confusing, it might help to write the formula for f' with empty boxes instead of "x", as we did in **Straight Forward Pre-Calculus.**
>
> $\quad\quad f(\boxed{}) = (\boxed{})^9 \quad\quad\quad f'(\boxed{}) = 9(\boxed{})^8$
>
> $\quad\quad g = 3x - 2 \quad\quad\quad\quad\quad\quad\quad g' = 3$

Then, to get $f'(g(x))$, we substitute $g(x)$, which is $3x-2$, into the empty boxes:

$$f'(g) = 9(\boxed{3x-2})^8$$

Therefore the Chain Rule formula gives us:

$(g') \cdot (f'(g))$

$= (3)\ 9(3x-2)^8$, or

$27(3x-2)^8$.

Examples:

a. Find the slope of the tangent to line $y = \cos^2 x$ at $x = 1$.

b. Find the slope of the tangent to line $y = \cos(x^2)$ at $x = 1$.

Solutions:

a. First, remember that $\cos^2 x$ means $(\cos x)^2$. Therefore, $\cos^2 x$ can be expressed as the composition $f(g)$ where:

$f = x^2$ $f' = 2x$

$g = \cos x$ $g' = -\sin x$

Therefore, $f'(g) = 2\cos x$, and the Chain Rule formula gives us:

$(-\sin x)\ (2\cos x) = -2\sin x \cos x$.

Now we can substitute $x = 1$, and we get:

$(-2)(0.8415)(0.5403) = -0.9093$.

NOTE: We could also have solved this problem by expressing $\cos^2 x$ as $(\cos x)(\cos x)$, and then using the product formula. If we had done so, the answer would have been the same. The reader is invited to verify this fact for herself/himself.

b. This function is composed of the same two simpler functions as Part a, but the f and the g are reversed:

$f = \cos x$ $f' = -\sin x$

$g = x^2$ $g' = 2x$

So the Chain Rule formula, $(g') \cdot (f'(g))$, gives us:

$2x(-\sin(x^2))$, or $-2x \sin(x^2)$.

Substituting $x = 1$, we get $(-2)(0.84147) = -1.68294$.

Notice that the two examples above had two different answers. It is important to know which function is f and which is g when expressing the original function as the composition f(g)!

Example:

Derive a general formula for the derivative of $(g(x))^n$ where $g(x)$ is any function at all, and n is a nonzero number.

Solution:

We apply the Chain Rule with f, f′, g, g′ as follows:

$$f = x^n \qquad\qquad f' = nx^{n-1}$$
$$g = g \qquad\qquad g' = g'$$
(What else?)

Then the Chain Rule formula gives us:

$$(g') \cdot (ng^{n-1}).$$

The formula derived in the example above come up so often that it is sometimes given its own name:

General Power Rule

$$\frac{d}{dx}(g(x))^n = g'(x) \cdot n(g(x))^{n-1}$$

In words: If you have an expression in parentheses, raised to a power, and you want the derivative, then:

1. Bring the exponent down in front.
2. Reduce the exponent by 1.
3. Multiply by the derivative of the expression inside the parentheses.

The General Power Rule provides an alternative to the quotient rule when differentiating functions of the form $\frac{k}{(g(x))^n}$.

Example:

Let $f(x) = \dfrac{3}{2x^2+3x-1}$.

Find $f'(-2)$.

Solution:

We can rewrite the function as $f(x) = 3(2x^2 + 3x - 1)^{-1}$, and then use the General Power Rule with $g(x) = 2x^2 + 3x - 1$ and $n = -1$:

$g(x) = 2x^2 + 3x - 1$, so $g'(x) = 4x + 3$.

The General Power Rule formula then says that:

$f'(x) = -3(4x+3)(2x^2+3x-1)^{-2}$

(Remember that the 3 at the front is there because when a function is multiplied by a constant, the derivative is multiplied by the same constant—see Formula 4 in Part 3 of this Chapter)

Simplifying and writing the function in the original form, we have:

$$f'(x) = \frac{-12x-9}{(2x^2+3x-1)^2}$$

Now we substitute $x = -2$ into $f'(x)$, and we get:

$f'(-2) = 15$.

Most people believe this is an easier procedure than using the quotient rule.

Once we have the Chain Rule available to us, it is even more important to be careful to identify the <u>basic form</u> of a function before beginning the differentiation process:

Examples:

a. Find the derivative of $\frac{\tan(4-5x)}{3x+2}$.

b. Find the derivative of $\tan\left(\frac{4-5x}{3x+2}\right)$.

Solutions:

a. The basic form of the function is that it is the quotient of two functions. One of the two component functions happens to be the composition of two functions. Therefore, we set up our usual 2-by-2 matrix with the intention of making the proper substitutions into the quotient rule:

$$f = \tan(4-5x) \qquad f' = ?$$
$$g = 3x+2 \qquad g' = 3$$

f is a composition of the two functions f_1 and g_1, where $f_1 = \tan x$, and $g_1 = 4 - 5x$. So we need the Chain Rule to get f' in the matrix above. The Chain Rule (verify this for yourself!) gives $f' = -5\sec^2(4 - 5x)$. So our matrix is now:

$$f = \tan(4 - 5x) \qquad\qquad f' = -5\sec^2(4 - 5x)$$
$$g = 3x + 2 \qquad\qquad\qquad g' = 3$$

Substituting into the quotient rule, we get our final answer:

$$\frac{(-15x-10)\sec^2(4-5x) - 3\tan(4-5x)}{(3x+2)^2}.$$

b. The basic form of this function is that it is the composition of two functions. One of the two component functions is a quotient, but the overall function is not a quotient. So we set up our matrix with the intention of substituting the proper expressions into the Chain Rule formula:

$$f = \tan x \qquad\qquad\qquad f' = \sec^2 x$$
$$g = \frac{4-5x}{3x+2} \qquad\qquad g' = \frac{-22}{(3x+2)^2}$$

(We filled in the g' expression by using the quotient rule, since g is a quotient).

Substituting into the Chain Rule formula, we get the answer:

$$\frac{-22}{(3x+2)^2} \sec^2\!\left(\frac{4-5x}{3x+2}\right)$$

CHAIN RULE–Second Version

If $u = f(x)$, then of course the value of u depends upon the value of x. If, in turn, $y = g(u)$, then the value of y depends upon the value of u. But since u depends on x, that means that the value of y also depends upon x. Therefore, a change in x causes a change in y, so we should be able to find the rate of change of y with respect to x; or in other words, $\frac{dy}{dx}$. The formula for this situation is given by the following rule:

Suppose $u = g(x)$, and
$$y = f(u).$$

Then $\dfrac{dy}{dx} = \dfrac{dy}{du}\dfrac{du}{dx}.$

This is just another way of expressing the Chain Rule, since $y = f(u) = f(g(x))$, so $\frac{du}{dx} = g'(x)$, and $\frac{dy}{du} = f'(u) = f'(g(x))$. However, it is easiest for most people to just memorize the two rules as separate rules.

Example:

Let $u = 4x^2 - 5$ and $y = \frac{2u+1}{2-3u}$.

Find $\frac{dy}{dx}$.

Solution:

There are two possible methods. We can use the second version of the Chain Rule above, or we can substitute $4x^2 - 5$ for u in the formula for y and then differentiate.

Method 1: $\frac{du}{dx} = 8x$, and $\frac{dy}{du} = \frac{7}{(2-3u)^2}$ (the quotient rule). The Chain Rule, second version, says that:

$$\frac{dy}{dx} = \frac{dy}{du}\frac{du}{dx} = \left(\frac{7}{(2-3u)^2}\right)8x = \frac{56x}{(2-3u)^2}.$$

Then, we substitute $u = 4x^2 - 5$, and get:

$$\frac{dy}{dx} = \frac{56x}{(2-3(4x^2-5))^2} = \frac{56x}{(17-12x^2)^2}.$$

Method 2: $y = \frac{2u+1}{2-3u}$; by substituting $u = 4x^2 - 5$, we have $y = \frac{8x^2-9}{17-12x^2}$. Then, by using the quotient rule, we get:

$$\frac{dy}{dx} = \frac{272x-192x^3-(-192x^3+216x)}{(17-12x^2)^2} = \frac{56x}{(17-12x^2)^2}.$$

Notice that we got the same answer using both methods, as we should. HOWEVER: The second method can be nearly unworkable if the functions involved are complicated enough. So it is necessary to know the first method well.

Derivatives. Exercise 8. The Chain Rule.

1. Let $f(x) = \cos(2x - 5)$. Find $f'(x)$.

2. Let $f(x) = \sin(x^2 - 5x)$. Find $f'(0)$.

3. Find the equation of the tangent line of $y = \tan(\frac{3x}{4})$ at $x = \pi$.

4. Locate all x values, $0 \le x \le \pi$, where the graph of $y = 3x^2 - \cos(3x^2)$ has a horizontal tangent line.

5. Find $\frac{d}{dx}(5x^8 - 2x + 3\sec x)^4$.

66

6. Find all x-values, with $0 \le x \le 2\pi$, such that the graph of $y = 2\sin^3 x$ has a horizontal tangent.

7. Find $g'(2)$ if $g(x) = \dfrac{4}{(4x^2-3x-9)^{10}}$.

8. Find the equation of the tangent line to $y = (4x^2 - 3x - 8)^5$ at $x = 2$.

9. Find $s'(t)$ if $s(t) = \tan(4x^2 \sin x)$.

10. Find $\dfrac{d}{dx}(\sin x \tan(4x^2))$.

11. Find the derivative of $\left(\dfrac{2x-3}{3x+5}\right)^6$.

12. Find the slope of the tangent line to $y = \dfrac{(2x-3)^6}{3x+5}$ at $x = -2$.

13. Find $f'(x)$ if $f(x) = \sin[(7 - 2x^2)^5]$.

14. Find the equation of the tangent line to $y = \sin^5(7 - 2x^2)$ at $x = 1$. Use at least 5 decimal places for each value.

15. If $u = \cos x$ and $y = \cos u$, find $\dfrac{dy}{dx}$ in terms of x.

16. Find $\dfrac{dy}{dx}$ in terms of x if $w = 2x^3 + 3x^2 + 4x + 5$, and $y = \dfrac{2w+1}{2w-1}$.

Part 9 — Derivatives of Logarithmic and Exponential Functions

The general properties of logarithmic and exponential functions were covered in **Straight Forward Pre-Calculus**. Here we will define an exponential function more broadly, and say that an exponential function is a function of the form

$$f(x) = b^{g(x)},$$

where b is some positive number (called the *base* of the exponential function), and g(x) might be any function at all.

Recall that the number e, which is equal to approximately 2.718281828, is used frequently in scientific and mathematical applications. One of the most important reasons for using e as a base is something we discovered in Problem 14 in the exercise for Part 1 of this chapter (page 32), and which was referred to again in an example in Part 2 (page 34):

$$\dfrac{d}{dx}(e^x) = e^x$$

By using the Chain Rule, we can find the derivatives of any exponential function with base e.

Example:

Find a general formula for the derivative of $e^{g(x)}$.

Solution:

We use the Chain Rule with:

$$f = e^x \qquad\qquad f' = e^x$$
$$g = g(x) \qquad\qquad g' = g'(x)$$

Substituting into the Chain Rule formula, we get:

$$g'(x) \cdot e^{g(x)}.$$

In words:

To differentiate an exponential function with base e, multiply the function by the derivative of the exponent. NOTICE THAT THE EXPONENT ITSELF DOES NOT CHANGE WHEN THE FUNCTION IS DIFFERENTIATED.

Examples:

Function	Derivative
e^{2x}	$2e^{2x}$
e^{2x-6}	$2e^{2x-6}$
$e^{\sin x}$	$\cos x \, e^{\sin x}$
e^{3x^2-5x}	$(6x - 5)e^{3x^2-5x}$
$e^{3x\sin x}$	$(3\sin x + 3x \cos x)e^{3x \sin x}$

(The product rule was used to get the derivative of 3x sin x for the last example.)

Example:

> Find a general formula for the derivative of $b^{g(x)}$ when b is any positive number and g is any function.
>
> Solution:
>
> To accomplish this, we remember that $b = e^{\ln(b)}$.
>
> Therefore, the function $b^{g(x)}$ can be rewritten as $\left(e^{\ln(b)}\right)^{g(x)}$, or $e^{(\ln b)(g(x))}$.
>
> Then we can use the formula for differentiating e-functions, remembering that $\ln(b)$ is a constant. The derivative is then:
>
> $$(\ln(b))(g'(x))e^{(\ln b)(g(x))},$$
>
> or $\quad (\ln(b))(g'(x))b^{g(x)}$.
>
> In other words, the rule is exactly the same as for $e^{g(x)}$, except that we also multiply the function by $\ln(b)$.

Example:

> If $f(x) = 5^{x^2+3x-4}$, find $f'(-4)$.
>
> Solution:
>
> The formula derived in the previous example says that we should multiply the original function (5^{x^2+3x-4}, in this case) by $\ln(5)$ times the derivative of the exponent. In this case, the result is:
>
> $$(\ln 5)(2x + 3)(5^{x^2+3x-4}).$$
>
> Substituting $x = -4$, the answer is:
>
> $$(\ln 5)(-5)(5^{x^2+3x-4})$$
> $$= (\ln 5)(-5)(5^0)$$
> $$= -5\ln(5), \text{ or approximately } -8.0472.$$

Derivatives of Logarithmic Functions

We define any function of the form

$$f(x) = \log_b (g(x)),$$

where b is any positive number except 1, and g(x) is any function, as a <u>logarithmic</u> function. The number b is called the *base* of the logarithmic function. Just as with the exponential functions, the base which makes differentiation easiest is e. Recall from **Straight Forward Pre-Calculus** that the usual notation for $\log_e x$ is ln x. It is a somewhat a startling fact that:

$$\frac{d}{dx}(\ln x) = \frac{1}{x}, \text{ or } x^{-1.}$$

By using the Chain Rule in a similar fashion to the method we used to find a formula for differentiating exponential functions with base e, we can find the following rule:

$$\frac{d}{dx}\ln(g(x)) = \frac{g'(x)}{g(x)}$$

In words:

To differentiate ln of any function g(x), form a fraction with the <u>derivative</u> of g(x) on top, and the original g(x) on the bottom. NOTICE THAT THE "ln" DISAPPEARS WHEN DIFFERENTIATING (unless g(x) involves ln also).

Examples:

Function	Derivative
$\ln(2x + 1)$	$\frac{2}{2x+1}$
$\ln(\tan x)$	$\frac{\sec^2 x}{\tan x}$, or $\sec x \csc x$
$\ln(8x^5 - 2x^3 + 6x - 1)$	$\frac{40x^4 - 6x^2 + 6}{8x^5 - 2x^3 + 6x - 1}$

Differentiating an ln function can often be simplified by using the following rules, which apply to all logs regardless of base:

$$\log_b(ac) = \log_b a + \log_b c$$
$$\log_b(\tfrac{a}{c}) = \log_b a - \log_b c$$
$$\log_b(a^c) = c \log_b a$$
$$\log_b(\tfrac{1}{a}) = -\log_b a$$

Examples:

Find the derivatives of:

   a. $\ln\left(\frac{3x+2}{4x-2}\right)$

   b. $\ln(\tan^3 x)$

   c. $\ln[(3x^5 - 2\sqrt{x} + 5x)(x^2 + 6)^4]$

Solution:

a. We could use our formula for an ln function with $g(x) = \frac{3x+2}{4x-2}$ and, in the process, find $g'(x)$ by using the quotient rule. But it's much easier to rewrite the function:

$$\ln\left(\frac{3x+2}{4x-2}\right) = \ln(3x + 2) - \ln(4x - 2).$$

Then we can easily differentiate term by term, according to the formula for differentiating ln functions:

$$\frac{3}{3x+2} - \frac{4}{4x-2}$$

b. Applying the rule of the log of a function to a power, we have:

$\ln(\tan^3 x) = 3\ln(\tan x)$. So the derivative we want is

$$\frac{3\sec^2 x}{\tan x}, \text{ or } 3\sec x \csc x.$$

c. By applying two rules successively, we break the original function down as follows:

$$\ln\left[(3x^5 - 2\sqrt{x} + 5x)(x^2 + 6)^4\right]$$

$$= \ln(3x^5 - 2\sqrt{x} + 5x) + \ln(x^2 + 6)^4$$

$$= \ln(3x^5 - 2\sqrt{x} + 5x) + 4\ln(x^2 + 6).$$

Once again, the differentiation step is now comparatively easy. The derivative is:

$$\frac{15x^4 - x^{-\frac{1}{2}} + 5}{3x^5 - 2\sqrt{x} + 5x} + \frac{8x}{x^2 + 6}$$

BIG TIME WARNING

A common stumbling block for calculus students is a function which includes a term like ln 3. Students can't figure out how to differentiate it. But ln 3 is a __constant__—it's equal to about 1.0986. Therefore the derivative of ln 3 is zero. The same thing applies to e raised to a __numerical__ power: $e^{2.6}$ is a constant whose derivative is zero.

Finally, the general rule for differentiating a log function whose base is other than e is:

$$\frac{d}{dx}\big(\log_b(g(x))\big) = \frac{g'(x)}{g(x)\cdot\ln(b)}$$

In other words, the rule is exactly the same as for ln(g(x)), except that we put ln(b) on the bottom of the fraction along with g(x).

The rule is derived by applying the base-changing formula:

$$\log_b(y) = \frac{\ln y}{\ln b}$$

to $\log_b\ (g(x))$.

A Note on the Domain of $\log_b$

Remember that the domain of $\log_b x$ is all positive numbers (zero is not in the domain). Therefore, a function such as ln(sin x) has a strange domain: $(0,\ \pi)$, $(2\pi,\ 3\pi)$ $(4\pi,\ 5\pi)$, etc., because those intervals are the only places where the sine function is positive. To avoid this problem, a function such as $\ln\big(|\sin x|\big)$ is seen fairly often. But adding the absolute value does not complicate the differentiation process, because $|g(x)|$ is always either g(x) itself or -g(x). For any x value of which $|g(x)| = -g(x)$, the derivative of $\ln\big(|g(x)|\big)$ would be:

$$\frac{-g'(x)}{-g(x)}$$

and the minus signs cancel out, leaving us with the same formula we use when there are no absolute value signs.

Derivatives. Exercise 9. Exponential and Logarithmic Functions.

In problems 1-24, find f'(x).

1. $f(x) = \log_3(5x^2 + 1)$

2. $f(x) = (5x^2 + 1)\ln(5x^2 + 1)$

3. $f(x) = e^{4x-2}$

4. $f(x) = e^{[(x^2 + 3x)(2x - \cos x)]}$

5. $f(x) = (x^2 - 4x - 3\ln(5 - 2x))^7$

6. $f(x) = \frac{\ln(3-2\tan x)}{4}$

7. $f(x) = \ln[3\sin x - 4x^3)^5]$

8. $f(x) = 2\ln(4x - 7x^{10})$

9. $f(x) = \ln[(x^3 + 2x^4 + 3x^5)(\sin x + \cos x + \tan x)]$

10. $f(x) = 3\sqrt{x^5} - 4\ln 2x + 5e^{x^2}$

11. $f(x) = \log_5(\frac{3}{x} + 2\cos x)$

12. $f(x) = \ln(\sin(4x^2 - 8x))$

13. $f(x) = 6^{7x^5-4x}$

14. $f(x) = e^{(7x^5 - 4x)^8}$

72

15. $f(x) = \dfrac{4e^{x^2} + 5\sec x}{6x - 8x^3}$

16. $f(x) = e^{4\tan x - 2x^5}$

17. $f(x) = e^{\cos^3 x}$

18. $f(x) = e^{6x^4}\left(3x^2 + 4\sin x - \dfrac{5x}{8}\right)$

19. $f(x) = 4^{2\tan x}$

20. $f(x) = \ln\left(\dfrac{3x^2 - 1}{4x + 1}\right)$

21. $f(x) = \cos(5\sqrt{x} - 2x^2 + e^{17x})$

22. $f(x) = e^{\left(\frac{5x-6}{6x+5}\right)}$

23. $f(x) = \dfrac{\ln(3x^2 + 5x + 2)}{3x^2 + 5x + 2}$

24. $f(x) = e^{\ln(2x-1)}$

25. Locate the x- and y-coordinates of all points where the graph of $y = 2xe^{x-5}$ has a horizontal tangent.

26. Find the first, second, third, and tenth derivatives of e^{2x-15}.

Part 10 | Logarithmic Differentiation

The formula for the derivative of $\ln(g(x))$ gives us a helpful method for differentiating complicated functions:

$$\frac{g'(x)}{g(x)} = \frac{d}{dx}(\ln(g(x))) \rightarrow g'(x) = (g(x))\frac{d}{dx}(\ln(g(x)))$$

The reason this formula is helpful is that $\ln(g(x))$ can be simplified by using the rules of logs mentioned previously in Part 9:

$$\ln(ab) = \ln\ a + \ln b$$

$$\ln\left(\frac{a}{b}\right) = \ln\ a - \ln b$$

$$\ln(a^b) = (b)\ln\ a$$

Once $\ln(g(x))$ has been broken into ln's of simpler functions, we can differentiate each individual ln more easily than the original $\ln(g(x))$.

In words, the derivative $g'(x)$ can be calculated by the following steps:

1. Take ln of g(x).

2. Break $\ln(g(x))$ into ln's of simpler functions by using the rules above.

3. Differentiate the results of Step 2.

4. Multiply the results of Step 3 by the original g(x).

The method described in these four steps is called logarithmic differentiation.

Examples:

Find the derivatives of the following functions:

a. $(2x - 3)^4(5x - 6)^7(8x - 9)^{10}$

b. $\dfrac{(\sin x - 2\cot x)^4(3x^6 - 4\sqrt{x^7} + 6)^9}{\sqrt{4x^5 - 6x^2 + 8}}$

c. $x^{\sin x}$

Solutions:

a. By taking the ln of the function and then simplifying, we get:

$$\ln\left[(2x - 3)^4(5x - 6)^7(8x - 9)^{10}\right]$$
$$= \ln\left[(2x - 3)^4\right] + \ln\left[(5x - 6)^7\right] + \ln\left[(8x - 9)^{10}\right]$$
$$= 4\ln(2x - 3) + 7\ln(5x - 6) + 10\ln(8x - 9).$$

Then we differentiate:

$$4\left(\frac{2}{2x-3}\right) + 7\left(\frac{5}{5x-6}\right) + 10\left(\frac{8}{8x-9}\right)$$
$$= \frac{8}{2x-3} + \frac{35}{5x-6} + \frac{80}{8x-9}$$

Finally, we multiply by the original function to get our answer:

$$(2x - 3)^4(5x - 6)^7(8x - 9)^{10}\left(\frac{8}{2x-3} + \frac{35}{5x-6} + \frac{80}{8x-9}\right)$$

b. Taking the ln of the function and simplifying, we get:

$$\ln\left[(\sin x - 2\cot x)^4\right] + \ln\left[(3x^6 - 4\sqrt{x^7} + 6)^9\right] - \ln\left[(4x^5 - 6x^2 + 8)^{\frac{1}{2}}\right]$$

$$= 4\ln(\sin x - 2\cot x) + 9\ln(3x^6 - 4\sqrt{x^7} + 6 - \frac{1}{2}\ln(4x^5 - 6x^2 + 8)$$

Then we differentiate:

$$\frac{4(\cos x + 2\csc^2 x)}{\sin x - 2\cot x} + \frac{9(18x^5 - 14\sqrt{x^5})}{3x^6 - 4\sqrt{x^7} + 6} - \left(\frac{1}{2}\right)\frac{20x^4 - 12x}{4x^5 - 6x^2 + 8}$$

$$= \frac{4\cos x + 8\csc^2 x}{\sin x - 2\cot x} + \frac{162x^5 - 126\sqrt{x^5}}{3x^6 - 4\sqrt{x^7} + 6} - \frac{5x^4 - 3x}{2x^5 - 3x^2 + 4}$$

Finally, we multiply by the original function to get our final answer:

$$\left(\frac{4\cos x + 8\csc^2 x}{\sin x - 2\cot x} + \frac{162x^5 - 126\sqrt{x^5}}{3x^6 - 4\sqrt{x^7} + 6} - \frac{5x^4 - 3x}{2x^5 - 3x^2 + 4}\right)\left(\frac{(\sin x - 2\cot x)^4(3x^6 - 4\sqrt{x^7} + 9)}{\sqrt{4x^5 - 6x^2 + 8}}\right)$$

c. This type of function (a function with an x in the function on the ground and another x in the exponent) can't be differentiated in any other way than by using logarithmic differentiation. We follow the same steps as in Examples a and b:

$$\ln(x^{\sin x}) = \sin x \ln x.$$

Then we differentiate, using the Product Rule for fg, with:

$$f = \sin x \qquad\qquad f' = \cos x$$
$$g = \ln x \qquad\qquad g' = \frac{1}{x}$$

And the product rule then gives us $\cos x \ln x + \frac{1}{x}\sin x$, or $\cos x \ln x + \frac{\sin x}{x}$.

Finally, we multiply by the original function and get:

$$\left(\cos x \ln x + \frac{\sin x}{x}\right)\left(x^{\sin x}\right)$$

Derivatives. Exercise 10. Logarithmic Differentiation.

In problems 1-6, find the derivative.

1. $(x^2 + x + 1)^6(9x^2 - 8x + 7)^5(6x - 5x^3 + 4x^2)^4$

2. $\dfrac{\sqrt{x^2 + x + 1}(9x^2 - 8x + 7)^5}{6x - 5x^3 + 4x^2}$

3. $\dfrac{(\sec x - 2\csc x + 3\cot x)^{18}(e^{3x} + 5x^2)^6}{(5x^5 - 3\ln x + 6x - 2)^9}$

4. x^x

5. $(\cos x)^{3x-1}$

6. $(\ln x)^{e^x}$

7. Differentiate $\frac{2x-1}{5x+4}$ two ways: with the quotient rule and with logarithmic differentiation. Then verify that the two answers are equal.

8. Differentiate $(2x - 1)(5x + 4)^2$ both by logarithmic differentiation and with the product and general power rules, and verify the equivalence of the answers.

Below we collect in a table all the important differentiation formulas presented in this chapter.

In the table, the letters f and g always stand for functions (of x), the letters b, k, m, and n always stand for numbers (constants), and the letter x always stands for the variable.

Function	Derivative
$f + g$	$f' + g'$
$f - g$	$f' - g'$
kf	kf'
mx	m
k	0
kx^n	nkx^{n-1}
fg	$f'g + g'f$ (product rule)
$\dfrac{f}{g}$	$\dfrac{f'g - g'f}{g^2}$ (quotient rule)
$\sin x$	$\cos x$
$\cos x$	$-\sin x$
$\tan x$	$\sec^2 x$
$\sec x$	$\sec x \tan x$
$\csc x$	$-\cot x \csc x$
$\cot x$	$-\csc^2 x$
$f(g)$ (composition)	$g' \cdot f'(g)$ (chain rule)
e^x	e^x
$e^{g(x)}$	$g'(x) \cdot e^{g(x)}$
$\ln x$	$\dfrac{1}{x}$
$\ln(g(x))$	$\dfrac{g'(x)}{g(x)}$
$(g(x))^n$	$n \cdot g'(x) \cdot (g(x))^{n-1}$ (general power rule)
b^x	$(\ln b) b^x$
$b^{g(x)}$	$(\ln b) g'(x) b^{g(x)}$
$\log_b x$	$\dfrac{1}{x \ln b}$
$\log_b(g(x))$	$\dfrac{g'(x)}{(\ln b) g(x)}$
$g(x)$ (any function)	$(\ln(g(x)))' \cdot g(x)$ (logarithmic differentiation)

Derivatives. Exercise 11. Summary.

In problems 1-32, find p'(t).

1. $p(t) = (e^7 \sin t)(3t^8 - \frac{1}{t})$

2. $p(t) = e^t$

3. $p(t) = t^{\frac{1}{t}}$

4. $p(t) = 4t^8 - 5t^{\frac{3}{4}} - \frac{7}{t^2} + 8\sqrt[3]{t}$

5. $p(t) = \cos(4t^6)$

6. $p(t) = 4\cos^6 t$

7. $p(t) = \log_4(3t^2 + 5t)$

8. $p(t) = \frac{\tan t}{14t - 6}$

9. $p(t) = e^{(3t^4 - \ln 7)}$

10. $p(t) = 12$

11. $p(t) = -\csc(2t)$

12. $p(t) = 4^{\sec t}$

13. $p(t) = (\ln 8)t$

14. $p(t) = \sec(4t)$

15. $p(t) = (\log_5 6)^t$

16. $p(t) = 6\ln t$

17. $p(t) = 8 - \cot t$

18. $p(t) = \log_{17} t$

19. $p(t) = e^5 - 4t^3$

20. $p(t) = e^t - 4t^3$

21. $p(t) = (\cos t) - \frac{4}{t^3}$

22. $p(t) = \ln\left|5t^5 + e^t\right|$

23. $p(t) = \ln 6 + 4\sqrt[5]{t}$

24. $p(t) = \ln t + 4\sqrt[5]{t}$

25. $p(t) = \sin(et)$

26. $p(t) = (e)\ln t$

27. $p(t) = 4(2t - 7)^{55}$

28. $p(t) = \tan\left(\sqrt{7t}\right)$

29. $p(t) = (e^t - \ln t)^{18}$

30. $p(t) = \cos\left(\frac{3t-4}{5t+6}\right)$

31. $p(t) = \frac{3\cos t - 4}{5t + 6}$

32. $p(t) = \left[t + \sin^5(3t^4 + 10t - 2)\right]^7$

Part 12 — Implicit Differentiation

If y is a function of x, we know how to get $\frac{dy}{dx}$ (the derivative of y with respect to x) as long as the function which defines y is given to us as an explicit formula involving x. However, there are equations involving x and y in which it is difficult or impossible to solve the equation for y as a function of x. These equations have graphs, and the graphs have slopes at various points, just as the graphs of functions do.

Examples:

a. The graph of the equation $x^2 + y^2 = 16$ is a circle of radius 4 with center at the origin. However, the equation does not define a function. If we try to solve the equation for y, we'll get a "plus or minus" on the other side.

b. The equation $2x^2y^5 - 5xy^3 - 3x + 4y = 28$ has a (probably very complicated) graph. The graph includes, for example the points (-2,1) and $(-\frac{28}{3}, 0)$. But the equation is difficult or impossible to solve for y.

Implicit differentiation is a tool which enables us to calculate the slopes of graphs of equations such as the ones in the two examples above. The idea of implicit differentiation is based on the assumption that, in a small neighborhood of a given point on a graph, y can be expressed as a function of x even though we might not know explicitly what the function is.

Therefore, at any given point, we are justified in assuming that $\frac{dy}{dx}$ exists, even though we don't know a formula for it. Therefore, we can differentiate, with respect to x, any expression involving x's and y's, *remembering that y is not just a variable*—it's a function of x. This last consideration requires us to use the Chain Rule, product rule, or quotient rule for expressions such as $3x^2y$, y^5, or $\frac{y}{2y-x}$.

Examples:

Differentiate the following expressions with respect to x:

a. $3x^2y$

b. y^5

c. $\frac{y}{2y-x}$

Solutions:

In what follows, we will use the less cumbersome notation y′ instead of $\frac{dy}{dx}$.

a. It is frequently helpful to rewrite the expression with the letter "y" in parentheses, as a reminder that y is considered a <u>function</u> of x, and not just a variable:
$$3x^2(y)$$
The expression in this problem is a <u>product</u> of two functions f and g, where:

$$f = 3x^2 \qquad\qquad f' = 6x$$

$$g = (y) \qquad\qquad g' = y'$$

Therefore, our answer is $f'g + g'f = 6xy + 3x^2y'$.

b. Rewriting the expression as $(y)^5$, we see that the expression calls for the general power rule, and the answer is $5y^4 y'$.

c. We rewrite the expression as $\dfrac{(y)}{2(y)-x}$, and use the quotient rule with:

$$f = (y) \qquad\qquad f' = y'$$

$$g = 2(y) - x \qquad\qquad g' = 2y' - 1$$

Substituting into the quotient rule, we get our answer:

$$\frac{y'(2y-x)-y(2y'-1)}{(2y-x)^2} = \frac{y-xy'}{(2y-x)^2}$$

Examples:

a. Find the slope of the circle $x^2 + y^2 = 16$ at the point $\left(\sqrt{7}, -3\right)$.

b. Find the equation of the line tangent to $2x^2y^5 - 5xy^3 - 3x + 4y = 28$, at point $(-2, 1)$.

Solutions:

a. If we differentiate both sides of the equation with respect to x (as in the previous examples), we get:

$$2x + 2yy' = 0.$$

Solving this equation for y', we get $y' = \dfrac{-x}{y}$.

Substituting $x = \sqrt{7}$ and $y = -3$, we find

$$y' = \frac{\sqrt{7}}{3}.$$

b. Rewriting the equation as $2x^2(y)^5 - 5x(y)^3 - 3x + 4(y) = 28$ and then differentiating with respect to x, we get:

$$10x^2y^4 y' + 4xy^5 - 15xy^2 y' - 5y^3 - 3 + 4y' = 0.$$

To solve this for y', we put all terms containing y' on the left, and all terms without y' on the right:

$$10x^2y^4 y' - 15xy^2 y' + 4y' = 5y^3 - 4xy^5 + 3.$$

Then we factor out the y' on the left-hand side:

$$(10x^2y^4 - 15xy^2 + 4)y' = 5y^3 - 4xy^5 + 3$$

Finally we divide both sides by the coefficient of y', solving for y':

$$y' = \frac{5y^3 - 4xy^5 + 3}{10x^2y^4 - 15xy^2 + 4}.$$

Now we can substitute x = -2 and y = 1, to get our slope:

$$\frac{5-4(-2)(1)+3}{10(4)(1)-15(-2)(1)+4} = \frac{16}{74} = \frac{8}{37}.$$

Last of all, we substitute x = -2, y = 1, m = $\frac{8}{37}$ into the point-slope formula, and we get the equation of the tangent line:

$$y - 1 = \frac{8}{37}(x + 2), \text{ or } y = \frac{8}{37}x + \frac{53}{37}.$$

Of course, this same general procedure can be used to differentiate any equation or expression with respect to any variable (let's say *t*), when some of the variables in the equation or expression are functions of *t*.

Example:

Suppose V, r and h are all functions of t. If $V = 2\pi rh + 2\pi r^2$, find $\frac{dV}{dt}$ in terms of r, h, $\frac{dr}{dt}$, and $\frac{dh}{dt}$.

Solution:

Since all three variables are functions of a fourth variable t, we rewrite the equation with parentheses around each variable:

$$(V) = 2\pi(r)(h) + 2\pi(r)^2.$$

We then differentiate both sides with respect to t. Remember that π is a <u>constant</u>, and gets treated just like a 5. Also, the term $2\pi(r)(h)$ is a product of two functions. The differentiated equation looks like this:

$$V' = 2\pi r'h + 2\pi rh' + 4\pi rr', \text{ or, in } \tfrac{d}{dt}\text{form :}$$

$$\frac{dV}{dt} = 2\pi\frac{dr}{dt}h + 2\pi r\frac{dh}{dt} + 4\pi r\frac{dr}{dt}.$$

Derivatives. Exercise 12. Implicit Differentiation.

1. Find y' in terms of x and y, when $x^2 - y^2 = 25$.

2. Find y' in terms of x and y, when $x^2 + y^2 = y$.

3. Find the slope of $x^2 + 2xy + y^2 = 25$ at any point at all.

4. Find the slope of $x^2 + 3xy + y^2 = -11$ at (3,-4).

5. Find the equation of the line tangent to $\frac{x}{x+y} = y^2 + 5y + 15x$ at (-1,2).

6. Find two points at which the curve $25x^2 + 9y^2 = 225$ has horizontal tangents.

7. Find two points at which the curve $25x^2 + 9y^2 = 225$ has vertical tangents.

8. Suppose x and y are both functions of t, that $x^2 + 2y^2 = 99$, and that $\frac{dy}{dt} = 3$, when x = -7 and y = 5. Then find $\frac{dx}{dt}$, when x = -7 and y = 5.

Part 13 | Differentiating Inverse Functions

Recall that g is the <u>inverse</u> function for f if f(g(x)) = x and g(f(x)) = x. Informally, g "undoes" the action of f. A commonly used notation for the inverse to f(x) is $f^{-1}(x)$.

Examples:

> The inverse of f(x) = 2x is g(x) = $\frac{1}{2}$x.
> The inverse of f(x) = x+8 is g(x) = x-8.
> The inverse of f(x) = x^2-1 is g(x) = $\sqrt{x+1}$, for x ≥ 0.

Another fact to remember is that not all functions have inverses. In order to have an inverse, f must be one-to-one—that is, any two different values of x must yield two different values of f(x). Another way of saying that is f(a) = f(b) only if a = b. The graphical equivalent of the one-to-one property is that the graph must pass the "horizontal line test": There can be no horizontal line which intersects the graph more than once.

If a function is not one-to-one and thus has no inverse, we can sometimes restrict the domain of that function so that the restricted function is one-to-one.

Example:

> The function of f(x) = x^2 is not one-to-one, because (for example) both f(2) and f(-2) are equal to 4. However, if we restrict the domain of f(x) to the interval (-∞,0), then the restricted version of f(x) is one-to-one, and has an inverse. That inverse is g(x) = $-\sqrt{x}$.

If f(x) is a one-to-one function, we can sometimes find the value of the derivative of the inverse even if we don't have an explicit formula for the inverse itself. The rule is:

> Let g(x) be the inverse function for f(x), and let c be a number such that f'(g(c)) is <u>not</u> equal to zero. Then:
>
> $$g'(c) = \frac{1}{f'(g(c))}.$$

81

Example:

Let $f(x) = x^3 + 2x$, and let $g(x)$ = the inverse function for $f(x)$. Find $g'(3)$.

Solution:

Note that $f(1) = 3$, which means that $g(3) = 1$. According to the formula above,
$$g'(3) = \frac{1}{f'(g(3))} = \frac{1}{f'(1)}.$$
Since $f'(x) = 3x^2 + 2$, and $f'(1) = 5$, we have $g'(3) = \frac{1}{5}$.

The formula for the derivative of an inverse function enables us to find derivatives for the inverse trigonometric functions. We will use the arctan function as an example, and give the derivatives of the other inverse trigonometric functions without showing their derivations in detail.

Example:

Find $\frac{d}{dx}(\tan^{-1} x)$.

Solution:

Recall that $\tan^{-1}x$ can be thought of as an angle whose tangent is x. If x is positive, then $\tan^{-1}x$ is represented by a first quadrant angle between 0 and $\frac{\pi}{2}$. If x is negative, the $\tan^{-1}x$ is represented by a fourth quadrant angle between $-\frac{\pi}{2}$ and 0. We will base our prodecure on a diagram which assumes that x is positive. However, the final answer would come out the same if we used a corresponding diagram for a negative x.

Since the tangent of $\tan^{-1}x$ is x, and since the tangent of any acute angle in a right triangle is the ratio of the opposite over the adjacent sides, we can draw tan x as the angle:

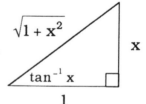

(The length of the hypotenuse was calculated by using the Pythagorean Theorem.)

The formula for the derivative of an inverse states that if $g(x)$ is the inverse of $f(x)$, then:

$$g'(x) = \frac{1}{f'(g(x))}.$$

For this problem, $f(x) = \tan x$, $g(x) = \tan^{-1}x$, and $f'(x) = \sec^2 x$. From the diagram, we can see that $\sec(\tan^{-1}x)$ is $\sqrt{1 + x^2}$ (hypotenuse over adjacent). Therefore,

$$g'(x) = \frac{1}{(\sqrt{1+x^2})^2} = \frac{1}{1+x^2}.$$

By using a similar approach, we can find the derivatives of the other 5 trigonometric functions. Those are left to the following exercise.

Derivatives. Exercise 13. Differentiating Inverse Functions.

1. Find $\frac{d}{dx}(\sin^{-1} x)$.

2. Find $\frac{d}{dx}(\arccos x)$.

3. Find $\frac{d}{dx}(\sec^{-1} x)$.

4. Find $\frac{d}{dx}(\operatorname{arccsc} x)$.

5. Find $\frac{d}{dx}(\cot^{-1} x)$.

6. Let $g(x)$ be the inverse of $f(x) = 2x^3 + 3x^2 + 6x - 8$. Find $g'(3)$.

7. Let $g(x)$ be the inverse of $\cos x - 2e^x$, for $-0.5 \le x$. Find $g'(-1)$.

8. Let $f(3) = 2$, $f'(3) = -2$, and g be the inverse of f. Find $g'(2)$.

Applications of Derivatives

So far, most of this book has been devoted to rules for finding limits and derivatives. There has been very little discussion about the reasons for using derivatives. Most of Chapter Three is concerned with the many kinds of problems which can be solved by using derivatives.

Part 1 Differentiability and Continuity

If a function f has a derivative, then f is said to be **differentiable**. If $f'(c)$ exists for a particular value c, then f is said to be differentiable at c. Not all functions are differentiable. Also, it is possible for a function to be differentiable for some values of x and not differentiable for other values. One of the most important theorems concerning differentiabilty is:

> If f(x) is not continuous at c, then f(x) is not differentiable at c.

> **BIG TIME WARNING**
>
> The converse of the theorem above is NOT true! Even if f(x) is continuous at c, then f(x) still might not be differentiable at c.

Example:

Let $f(x)=\begin{cases} x+7 & x < -5 \\ |x| & -5 \le x < 2 \\ x^2 - 3x + 4 & x \ge 2 \end{cases}$.

Then determine all points which f(x) is not continuous, and all points at which f(x) is not differentiable.

Solution:

f(x) is not continuous at x = -5, because $\lim_{x \to -5^-} f(x) = 2$, and $\lim_{x \to -5^+} f(x) = 5$. Therefore f(x) is not differentiable at x = -5. At x = 0, f(x) is continuous, because the absolute value function is continuous everywhere. However, the slope of the straight line connecting (x,f(x)) with (0,f(0)) is -1 whenever x is negative, and 1 whenever x is positive.

Therefore,

$$\lim_{x \to 0^-} \frac{f(0+h)-f(0)}{h} \quad \text{and} \quad \lim_{x \to 0^+} \frac{f(0+h)-f(0)}{h}$$

are different, so f'(0) does not exist, and f is not differentiable at 0.

Finally, we examine continuity and differentiability at x = 2. We see that:

$$\lim_{x \to 2^-} f(x) = 2, \quad \lim_{x \to 2^+} f(x) = 2, \text{ and } f(2) = 2.$$

Therefore, f is continuous at 2. Looking at derivatives, we see that the derivative of f(x) for 0 < x < 2 is 1 (the absolute value function has slope 1 for all x > 0). Consequently,

$$\lim_{h \to 0^-} \frac{f(2+h)-f(2)}{h} = 1.$$

Also, the derivative of x^2 - 3x + 4 is 2x - 3. If we substitute x = 2 into that expression, we get 1, giving us:

$$\lim_{h \to 0^+} \frac{f(2+h)-f(2)}{h} = 1.$$

Since the left-hand and right-hand limits of $\frac{f(2+h)-f(2)}{h}$ as h goes to zero are equal, the limit itself exists and is equal to 1, which means f'(2) = 1. f is therefore both continuous and differentiable at x = 2.

Determining Differentiability from Graphs

We already know that a function is continuous for any value of x where we can draw the graph right through the point without lifting the pencil from the paper. On the other hand, the function has a discontinuity wherever there is a break in the graph. Therefore, any break in the graph also indicates a point where the function is not differentiable.

A point at which a function is continuous but not differentiable will have an abrupt change of direction, or a "corner", such as the point (1, 5) in the accompanying graph. If the change of direction is "rounded", even a little bit, such as at the point (3, 1) in the graph, then the function is still differentiable at that point.

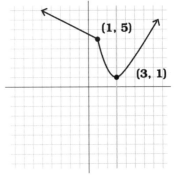

Applications of Derivatives. Exercise 1. Differentiabilty and Continuity.

In Problems 1-8, identify all discontinuities and points of non-differentiability.

1. $f(x) = \begin{cases} \sin x & x < 0 \\ x^2 & 0 \le x < 4 \\ 8x - 16 & 4 \le x < 5 \\ 7x - 10.9 & 5 \le x \end{cases}$

2. $g(x) = \begin{cases} \sin x & x < 0 \\ x^2 & 0 \le x < 4 \\ 8x - 16 & 4 \le x < 5 \\ x^2 - 2x + 9 & 5 \le x \end{cases}$

3. $h(x) = \begin{cases} 2 + \sin x & x < 0 \\ x^2 + x + 2 & 0 < 0 \\ 8x - 10 & 4 \le x < 5 \\ x^2 - 2x + 14 & 5 \le x \end{cases}$

4. $j(x) = \begin{cases} 2 + \sin x & x < 0 \\ x^2 + x + 2 & 0 < 0 \\ \frac{x}{x-4} & 4 \le x < 5 \\ 10 - x & 5 \le x \end{cases}$

5. $k(x) = \begin{cases} e^x & x < 0 \\ -2x & 0 \le x < 4 \\ x^2 - 10x + 16 & 4 \le x < 5 \\ x - 14 & 5 \le x \end{cases}$

6. $s(t) = \begin{cases} e^t & t < 0 \\ -2t & 0 \le t < 4 \\ t^3 - 6t^2 + 2t + 16 & 4 \le x < 5 \\ 10\sin(t - 5) + 7t - 34 & 5 \le x \end{cases}$

7.

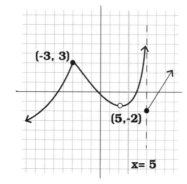

8.

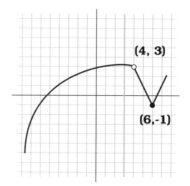

Part 2 **L'Hopital's Rule**

Among the hardest limits to compute are those involving fractions, in which both the numerator and denominator approach zero, or in which both the numerator and denominator approach plus or minus infinity. When the function is a rational function, we described (in Chapter 1, Part 7) a more or less complete procedure for calculating the limit. That procedure usually won't work, however, when the function includes trigonometric, logarithmic, exponential, or other more complicated expressions. But, one of the many properties which make a derivative useful is this: If we are trying to compute a limit, and we end up with zero over zero or infinity over infinity, we can replace the numerator and the denominator with their respective derivatives, and try again. This rule is called l'Hopital's Rule, named after the man who authored the first textbook ever written on differential calculus. More formally, the rule says this:

L'Hopital's Rule

Suppose either that $\lim\limits_{x \to a} f(x)$ and $\lim\limits_{x \to a} g(x)$ are both zero, or that $\lim\limits_{x \to a} f(x)$ and $\lim\limits_{x \to a} g(x)$ are both plus or minus infinity. Then,

$$\lim_{x \to a} \frac{f(x)}{g(x)} = \lim_{x \to a} \frac{f'(x)}{g'(x)}$$

if that second limit exists as a finite number or as plus or minus infinity. This fact also holds for left-hand or right-hand limits, as well as limits as x goes to plus or minus infinity.

Examples:

Find the following limits:

a. $\lim\limits_{x \to \infty} \dfrac{x^2 + 13x + 36}{x + 4}$

b. $\lim\limits_{x \to 0} \dfrac{\sin x}{x + \sin x}$

c. $\lim\limits_{x \to \infty} \dfrac{2x^3 + 10}{3x^3 - 500x^2 - 10^9}$

d. $\lim\limits_{x \to \infty} \dfrac{e^x - 17}{x^2}$

e. $\lim\limits_{x \to 0^+} (x \ln x)$

Solutions:

a. First, we must verify that l'Hopital's Rule applies. We let $f(x) = x^2 + 13x + 36$, and $g(x) = x + 4$. Substituting x = -4, we get f(-4) and g(-4) both = 0. So the rule applies, and we replace the original function with the fraction $\frac{2x + 13}{1}$. When we now substitute x = -4, the result is 5. So, by l'Hopital's Rule, the limit of the original function is also 5.

Note that the numerator, $x^2 + 13x + 36$, can be factored as $(x + 4)(x + 9)$. So, if we had used the Chapter 1 procedure, we would have reduced the fraction to a simple x + 9. Substituting x = -4 into that expression, we would have arrived at the same answer, 5.

b. If we substitute x = 0 into both the numerator and the denominator, we will get 0 in both cases. Therefore, l'Hopital's Rule applies, and we can look at the fraction formed by taking the derivatives of the numerator and denominator. That process gives us $\frac{\cos x}{1 + \cos x}$ which tells us that the limit we are looking for is $\frac{\cos 0}{1 + \cos 0} = \frac{1}{2}$.

c. As x approaches infinity, both the numerator and the denominator also approach infinity. If we use l'Hopital's Rule, it seems that we have made no progress, because the new function $\dfrac{6x^2}{9x^2-1000x}$, still goes to infinity over infinity. However, we can apply l'Hopital's Rule again, and again and again, until we finally get an expression whose limit we can compute. That process yields:

$$\frac{6x^2}{9x^2-1000x} \rightarrow \frac{12x}{18x-1000} \rightarrow \frac{12}{18} = \frac{2}{3}$$

The limit is $\frac{2}{3}$.

d. This problem again requires the application of l'Hopital's Rule more than once:

$$\frac{e^x-17}{x^2} \rightarrow \frac{e^x}{2x} \rightarrow \frac{e^x}{2} \rightarrow \infty .$$

A close look at this example will reveal that $\dfrac{e^x}{x^n}$ *always* approaches infinity as x approaches infinity, no matter how large n is. We just keep differentiating the top and bottom until the bottom is constant, while the e^x just remains e^x every time.

e. This function, as written, does not satisfy the conditions for l'Hopital's Rule. That rule requires a *fraction*, in which the numerator and denominator both have to approach the same value (either 0 or plus or minus infinity). However, when we have a product of two functions, one of which goes to zero and the other to plus or minus infinity, we can replace the product with a fraction of the kind we need:

$$x \ln x = \frac{\ln x}{\frac{1}{x}} = \frac{\ln x}{x^{-1}} .$$

Now we have the conditions for l'Hopital's Rule, because both the numerator and the denominator go to plus or minus infinity as x approaches zero (recall that ln x approaches negative infinity as x approaches zero). So we differentiate the top and bottom, which gives us:

$$\frac{\frac{1}{x}}{-x^{-2}} = \frac{x^{-1}}{-x^{-2}} = -(x^{-1+2}) = -x .$$

Substituting x = 0, we find that the limit we want is 0.

BIG-TIME WARNING

1. L'Hopital's Rule applies only when the limit has the form zero over zero or plus or minus infinity over infinity when the x value is

substituted. L'Hopital's Rule can <u>not</u> be used, for example, for limits such as $\lim\limits_{x\to 0} \dfrac{\cos x}{x}$.

2. Don't allow the use of l'Hopital's Rule to seduce you into the habit of *differentiating* a quotient by taking the derivative of the numerator over the derivative of the denominator. The process of differentiating a fraction requires the quotient rule, just as it always did before. The derivative of the numerator over the derivative of the denominator is pretty much useless for any purpose except using l'Hopital's Rule to find a limit.

Applications of Derivatives. Exercise 2. L'Hopital's Rule.

Find the limits.

1. $\lim\limits_{x\to -3} \dfrac{x+3}{x^2-9}$

2. $\lim\limits_{x\to \infty} \dfrac{x+3}{x^2-9}$

3. $\lim\limits_{x\to 0} \dfrac{\cos(2x+\frac{\pi}{2})}{x^3}$

4. $\lim\limits_{x\to 0} \dfrac{\cos(2x+\frac{\pi}{2})}{x^3-3x}$

5. $\lim\limits_{x\to 0} \dfrac{x}{\cos x}$

6. $\lim\limits_{x\to \frac{\pi}{2}} \dfrac{x\cos x}{\tan(x+\frac{\pi}{2})}$

7. $\lim\limits_{x\to 2} \dfrac{e^{3x-6}-1}{x^2+5x-14}$

8. $\lim\limits_{x\to \infty} \dfrac{e^{3x-6}-1}{x^2+5x-14}$

9. $\lim\limits_{x\to \infty} \dfrac{\cos(x-\frac{\pi}{2})}{2x}$

10. $\lim\limits_{x\to \infty} \dfrac{\ln(1+\frac{2}{x})}{(-\frac{3}{x})}$

Part 3 Maxima and Minima

As we mentioned in Part 6 of Chapter 2, derivatives can help us to locate the values of x for which a function is at its maximum or minimum values. In this section, we will make the notion of maximum and minimum more precise. We will also precisely state the relationship between maximum and minimum points, and derivatives. We will sometimes use the word "extremum" to mean either a maximum or a minimum. The plurals of extremum, maximum, and minimum are extrema, maxima, and minima respectively.

Formal Definition of Extreme Points:

A function f has a <u>relative maximum</u> at c if there is some open interval I which contains c and for which f(x) ≤ f(c) for every x in I.

A function f has a <u>relative minimum</u> at c if there is some open interval I which contains c and for which f(c) ≤ f(x) for every x in I.

A relative maximum or minimum is sometimes referred to as a local extremum.

A function f has an <u>absolute maximum</u> at c if f(x) ≤ f(c) for every x in the domain of f.

A function f has an <u>absolute minimum</u> at c if f(c) ≤ f(x) for every x in the domain of f.

Graphical Description of Relative and Absolute Extrema:

f has a relative minimum at a point which lies at the bottom of a "valley" on a graph (the graph must go up from that point on <u>both</u> sides), and a relative maximum at any point which is at the top of a hill.

f has an absolute maximum at the highest point on the entire graph. If two or more points are "tied" for that honor, then all of them represent absolute maxima. Similarly, f has an absolute minimum at the lowest point or points on the entire graph.

Example:

In the graph at the right, the point (-5, -2) is the lowest point anywhere on the graph. Therefore f(-5) = -2 is less than f(x) for any other value of x in the domain of f, which means f has an absolute minimum at -5. f also has a relative minimum at x = -5, because f(-5) will be less than f(x) for any value of x in any open interval I we care to choose which contains -5 —for example, (-6, -4).

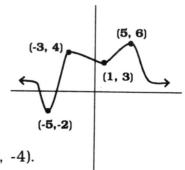

The point (1, 3) represents a <u>relative</u> minimum for f, because if we look only at the part of the graph which covers the interval (0, 2) (*left to right!*), then we can see that the point (1, 3) is the lowest point on the graph within that interval. So f has a relative minimum at -1.

Using the same reasoning as explained above, we will see that f has a relative maximum at -3, and both a relative and an absolute maximum at 5.

Two Points Require Clarification:

1. There is no law requiring a function to have any of the varieties of extrema we have discussed here. (Recall from Chapter 1, Part 8, however, that a function which is <u>continuous on a closed interval</u> must have both an (absolute) maximum and mimimum on that interval.)

2. It is possible to have an absolute extremum which is not a relative extremum. A look at the definition shows that if f has an absolute but not relative maximum or minimum at c, then there must be no open interval containing c inside the domain of f. That would occur, for example, if c were an endpoint of the domain. It is worth pointing out that in such cases, the <u>derivative</u> (f′) would be c. undefined at c, because f′is the limit of the slopes <u>on both sides</u> of In order to compute the limit, f must be defined for some distance to both the left and right of c, which means in some open interval containing c.

Example:

The function graphed here has an absolute mimimum at -5, but that is not a relative minimum because there is no open interval containing -5 which lies within the domain of the function. The function does have a relative minimum at 2 and a relative maximum at -2, but there is no absolute maximum because the function approaches the value 8 from below without ever getting there, as x goes to infinity. Note that the absence of an absolute maximum does not violate the theorem from Chapter 1 referred to above, because (-5, ∞) is not a closed interval.

"Maximum *at*" vs "Maximum Value *of*":

When we say "f has a maximum *at* 6", we mean that f reaches its maximum value when <u>x</u> = 6. If we say "the maximum value of f is 6", we mean that there is a number c for which f(c) = 6, and that f(x) is never any more than 6 no matter what other number we use for x. If the point (8, -4) is the highest point on the graph of f(x), that means that f has a maximum *at* 8, and that the maximum *value* for f is -4. Similar comments apply to minima.

The relationship between derivatives and extrema was mentioned informally in Chapter 2, Part 6. Here we make the relationship precise:

If f has an extremum at c, then either f′(c) = 0 or f′(c) is undefined.

A proof of the preceding theorem can be found in most standard calculus textbooks.

The preceding theorem means that when we are searching for extreme values of a function, we can restrict our search to x values of the following kinds:

a. values where the derivative is zero;
b. values where the derivative is undefined (of course, the original function must be defined at such values).

If c is a value which lies inside an open interval which is entirely contained in the domain of f, and if f(c) satisfies either condition (a) or condition (b) above, then c is called a *critical value* for f. The theorem above, then, says that any relative extremum of f must occur at a critical value for f.

BIG-TIME WARNING

Not all critical values give us relative extrema! 0 is a critical value for $f(x) = x^3$, since the derivative of x^3 is $3x^2$, which $= 0$ when $x = 0$. But x^3 has no maximum or minimum at $x = 0$.

Identifying Maximum and Minimum Points:

Identifying the critical points of f provides us with a list of candidates for extreme points. To determine which, if any, of the candidates are actually extrema, there are two methods. The first method was discussed in Chapter 2, Part 6, and is called the **First Derivative Test**. For the time being, <u>we will assume that f is continuous on its entire domain</u>. We perform the following steps for each critical value of c:

1. Find out whether $f'(x)$ is positive or negative for x values slightly less than c.

2. Do the same thing for x values slightly greater than c.

3. If the answer to #1 is positive, and #2 is negative, then f has a relative maximum at c.

4. If the answer to #1 is negative, and #2 is positive, then f has a relative minimum at c.

5. If the answer to #1 and #2 are both negative or both positive, then f does not have a relative extremum at c.

NOTE: When we talk about "values slightly less than (or greater than) c", we mean test any value close enough to c so that there is no *other* critical value between c and the value you are using.

For each value c which is an endpoint of the domain (and therefore does not lie inside an open interval contained in the domain), we take the following steps:

1. If c is a left-hand endpoint, find out whether f'(x) is positive or negative for x values slightly greater than c.

2. If the answer to #1 is plus, then c is an <u>endpoint minimum</u> and a potential absolute minimum.

3. If the answer to #1 is minus, then c is an <u>endpoint maximum</u> and a potential absolute maximum.

4. If c is a right-hand endpoint, find out whether f'(x) is positive or negative for x values slightly less than c.

5. If the answer to #1 is plus, then c is an endpoint maximum and a potential absolute maximum.

6. If the answer to #1 is minus, then c is an endpoint minimum and a potential absolute minimum.

We will discuss later the additional steps to be taken when the function has points of discontinuity.

Example:

Find all relative and absolute extrema of the function
$f(x) = x^4 - 6x^2 + 8x - 3$.

Solution:

$f'(x) = 4x^3 - 12x + 8 = 4(x - 1)^2 (x + 2)$ (the factoring was done with the help of the Rational Zeros Theorem from the **Straight Forward Pre-calculus** book).

The zeros of f'(x) are 1 and -2.

The domain of both f(x) and f'(x) are both all real numbers, so we have no possible extreme values at points not in the domain of f', or at the points not contained in an open interval which lies inside the domain. So our only two candidates for maxima and minima are -2 and 1.

f'(-3) = -64, and f'(-1) = 16. Therefore, f has a minimum at x = -2.

f'(0) = 8, and f'(2) = 16. So, by step #5 on page 92, f does not have an extreme point at x = 1. In particular, f is increasing (from left to right) as x approaches 1 from the left, and continues to increase as x goes away from 1 to the right (that's because f'(x) is positive in both places).

A number line showing the sign of f'(x) throughout its domain will look like this:

The number line shows that f decreases as x goes from -∞ to -2, and then increases forever as x goes from -2 to ∞. Therefore, f must have an absolute as well as relative minimum at x = -2, because the graph of f(x) goes up in both directions from the point where x = -2, and never turns around to come back down. On the other hand, since f and f' are both polynomials and continuous for all real numbers, any value in the domain of f is also in an open interval which lies entirely within the domain of f (for example, (-∞, ∞)!). So the only absolute extrema will have to be relative extrema also. Since we don't have any relative maxima (-2 and 1 were the only possibilities), f has no absolute maximum.

Example:

Find all relative and absolute maxima and minima for the function $f(x) = -3x^4 - 8x^3 + 48x^2 - 37$.

Solution:

$$f'(x) = -12x^3 - 24x^2 + 96x$$
$$= -12x(x + 4)(x - 2).$$

So the critical values are -4, 0 and 2.

$f'(-5) = 420$ and $f'(-3) = -180$, which means f has a relative maximum at x = -4.

$f'(-3) = -180$ and $(1) = 60$, which means f has a relative minimum at x = 0.

$f'(1) = 60$ and $f'(3) = -252$, which means f has a relative maximum at x = 2.

f(x) decreases forever as x approaches ∞, and also decreases forever as x goes <u>backward</u> toward -∞. Since f(x) is a polynomial, this means the graph of f(x) will plunge down to -∞ at both ends, which means there can be no absolute minimum.

On the other hand, f(x) must have an absolute maximum at either -4 or 2, because those are the only two relative maxima, and the function does not increase without limit anywhere. We find out which of the two gives the absolute maximum simply by comparing the values of f(x) at x = -4 and x = 2:

$$f(-4) = 475$$
$$f(2) = 43$$

Since f(-4) is greater than f(2), f(x) has both an absolute and a relative maximum at x = -4. The absolute maximum value of f(x) is 475, which is f(-4).

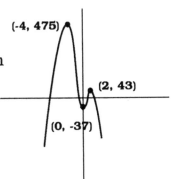

Example:

Find all relative and absolute extrema for the function:

$$f(x) \begin{cases} x^{\frac{2}{3}} + 1 & -8 \le x < 1 \\ x^2 - 8x + 9 & 1 \le x < 8 \end{cases}.$$

Solution:

First note that f is continuous at 1 because $\lim\limits_{x \to 1^-} f(x)$, $\lim\limits_{x \to 1^+} f(x)$, and f(1) are all equal to 2.

We calculate the derivative f'(x), and we get:

$$f'(x) \begin{cases} \dfrac{2}{3} x^{-\frac{1}{3}} = \dfrac{2}{3x^{\frac{1}{3}}} & -8 < x < 1 \\ 2x - 8 & 1 < x < 8 \end{cases}$$

Note that f' is undefined at -8 and at 1, even though f itself is defined at those values. This is because the limit of the slopes from the left is not defined in the case of -8, and the limit of the slopes from the left is different from the limit of the slopes on the right in the case of 1.

Also, f'(0) is undefined, because x = 0 would give us zero in the denominator.

The only solution to f'(x) = 0 is x = 4. So our critical values are -8, 0, 1, and 4.

By looking at the signs of f'(x) on the intervals defined by the critical points, we get the following number line:

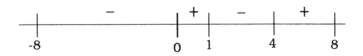

The number line tells us that we have relative minima at 0 and 4, and a relative maximum at 1. There is an endpoint maximum at -8. There is no extremum of any kind at x = 8, because 8 is not in the domain of the function at all.

To find the absolute minimum, we calculate:

$$f(0) = 1$$
$$f(4) = -7$$

Since f(4) is less than f(0), f has an absolute minimum of -7 at 4. To find the absolute maximum, we look at three facts:

$$f(-8) = 5$$
$$f(1) = 2$$
$$\lim_{x \to 8^-} f(x) = 9.$$

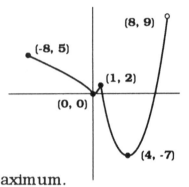

Although 8 is not in the domain of f, the fact that $\lim_{x \to 8^-} f(x)$ is 9 means that the values of f get very close to 9 as x approaches 8. Since 9 is greater than the values of f at the relative maximum at 1 and the endpoint maximum at -8, f does not have an absolute maximum.

When f is not continuous on its entire domain, we break the domain up into continuous pieces and treat each piece in the same manner we treated the functions in the examples above. If there is a single isolated value at which the function is defined but not continuous, we treat that one point on its own to determine whether it is an extreme point.

Example:

Find all relative and absolute extrema of the function

$$g(x) = \begin{cases} x^{\frac{2}{3}} & -8 \le x < 1 \\ -28.5 & x = 1 \\ x^2 - 8x + 9 & 1 < x < 8 \end{cases}$$

Solution:

This function is identical to the one in the previous example, except that now f is not continuous at 1. By looking at the interval [-8,1) on which f is continuous, we get the same relative minimum at 0 and endpoint maximum at -8 as last time. Looking at the interval (1,8), we again see a relative minimum at 4. However, the point (1,-28.5) must be considered on its own, since 1 is not part of any interval on which f is continuous. Since $\lim_{x \to 1^-} f(x)$ and $\lim_{x \to 1^+} f(x)$ are both 2, and -28.5 is less than 2, we see that f has a relative minimum at 1. In fact, since -28.5 is smaller than the relative minima at 0 and 4, f has an absolute minimum at 1. To sum up:

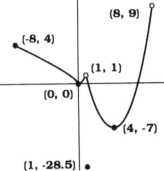

f has a relative minimum of 0 at 0 and a relative minimum of -7 at 4.

f has a relative and absolute minimum of -28.5 at 1.

f has an endpoint maximum at 4 at -8, but no absolute maximum (for the same reason as before).

The second method of determining relative extrema is often easier than the first derivative test, but it doesn't always work. The method is based on the following facts:

Second Derivative Test

1. If $f'(c) = 0$ and $f''(c)$ is positive, then f has a relative minimum at c.

2. If $f'(c) = 0$ and $f''(c)$ is negative, then f has a relative maximum at c.

3. If $f'(c) = 0$ and $f''(c) = 0$, then the second derivative test is inconclusive.

The statements above make sense if we recall the interpretations of the first and second derivatives given in the last chapter. If $f'(c) = 0$ and $f''(c)$ is positive, the graph must have a horizontal tangent and be concave up at c, like this:

On the other hand, if $f'(c) = 0$ and $f''(c)$ is negative, the graph must have a horizontal tangent and be concave down at c. The picture must then look like this:

The second derivative test tells us that if we have found the zeros of the first derivative, we can identify the relative maxima and mimima by following these steps:

1. For each zero c of $f'(x)$, calculate $f''(c)$.

2. If $f''(c)$ is negative, then f has a relative maximum at c.

3. If $f''(c)$ is positive, then f has a relative minimum at c.

4. If $f''(c) = 0$ or $f''(c)$ is undefined, then we must go back to the first derivative test in order to decide whether f has a relative maximum, a relative minimum, or neither at c.

5. For any critical value c for which $f'(c)$ is undefined, we must still use the first derivative test to find the nature of the point $(c, f(c))$.

97

Example:

> Find all absolute and relative extrema of the function:
>
> $$f(x) = 3x^5 - 5x^3 + 2.$$
>
> Solution:
>
> $$\begin{aligned} f'(x) &= 15x^4 - 15x^2 \\ &= 15x^2(x^2-1) \\ &= 15x^2(x+1)(x-1) \end{aligned}$$ which is defined everywhere, so that our critical values are -1, 0, and 1.
>
> $$f''(x) = 60x^3 - 30x,$$
> so that
> $f''(-1) = -30$, which means f has a relative maximum at -1,
> $f''(1) = 30$, which means f has a relative minimum at 1, and
> $f''(0) = 0$, which means we will need the first derivative test to determine the nature of the graph for f at $x = 0$.
>
> $f'(-0.5)$ and $f'(0.5)$ both $= -2.8125$, so the first derivative test shows that f does not have a relative (or absolute) extremum at $x = 0$.
>
> Since f is a polynomial of odd degree whose highest power term is positive, we know that $f(x)$ decreases without bound as x approaches negative infinity, and increases without bound as x approaches positive infinity. Therefore both of the extrema we found are relative but not absolute. To sum up:
>
> f has a relative maximum at -1, and a relative minimum at 1.

Applications of Derivatives. Exercise 3. Maxima and Minima.

In each case, identify all extrema and classify each as a maximum or minimum, and relative, absolute, or endpoint. When an interval is given after the function, the interval is the domain.

1. $x^4 - 8x^3 - 270x^2$

2. $x^3 - 9x + 1$

3. $3x^4 + 16x^3 + 12x^2 - 36x + 5$

4. $x^2 + \frac{2}{x} \left[\frac{1}{2}, 2\right]$

5. $\frac{6}{x^2 - 2x - 14}$

6. $\sqrt{49 - 9x^2}$ Hint : First find the domain.

7. $\sqrt{49 - 9x^2} \left(-\frac{7}{3}, \frac{7}{3}\right)$

8. $x - 2\cos x \left[-\pi, \pi\right]$

9. $x - 2\cos x \left(-\pi, \pi\right)$

10. $xe^{-2x} \left[0, \infty\right)$

11. $(x - 3)^{\frac{3}{5}}$

12. $2\sin x + \cos 2x \left[0, 2\pi\right]$

Part 4

Curve Sketching

Our knowledge of the roles played by the first and second derivatives of f(x) enable us to draw much more accurate graphs of functions than we could do without calculus. In Part 6 of Chapter 2, we saw that the signs of f'(a) and f"(a) determine whether a graph is increasing or decreasing, and whether the graph is concave up or down, at the point on the graph where x = a. In fact, a knowledge of the material in that section is almost all we need to know to draw an accurate graph of a function which is continuous and has no asymptotes. (Roughly speaking, any combination of polynomials, exponentials, sines, and cosines, with no denominators containing x's, will fall into this category.) The procedure is:

1. Determine the zeros and undefined points of f'(x) and f"(x). We will refer to those x values as "interesting numbers."

2. Divide a number line up into intervals whose endpoints are the interesting numbers from Step #1, and determine the signs of both f' and f" on each interval, as discussed in Chapter 2, Part 6.

3. Calculate the value of f at each interesting number, and plot the corresponding point on the graph. If there are any other numbers for which it is *easy* to calculate the value of f, then plot a few of those points too.

4. For the intervals between the interesting points, and at the far left and far right, choose the proper graph shape based on the signs of f' and f", by using the diagram below. Then connect the graph together by drawing the correct shapes between the points already plotted.

Example:

Sketch the graph of f(x) = x⁴ - 32x² + 31.

Solution:

First we find $f'(x) = 4x^3 - 64x = 4x(x^2-16)$
$f"(x) = 12x^2 - 64 = 4(3x^2-16)$

so that the zeros of f' are -4, 0, and 4, and the zeros of f" $-\frac{4}{\sqrt{3}}$ and $\frac{4}{\sqrt{3}}$, which are approximately -2.3 and 2.3.

When we draw a number line for f' and test the sign of f' on each interval, we get this:

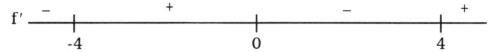

Doing the same thing for the sign of f", we get:

Now, when we put the two number lines together with all of the interesting points, we get:

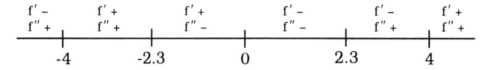

Now, to plot the interesting points on the graph, we calculate:

f(-4) = -225
f(-2.3) = -111   (approximately)
f(0) = 31
f(2.3) = -111   (again approximately)
f(4) = -225

Therefore, we plot the points:

(-4, -225)
(-2.3, -111)
(0, 31)
(2.3, -111)
(4, -225)

We could plot the point (1,0) also, since it is fairly easy to calculate.

Finally we connect the interesting points with graph pieces shaped according to the signs of f' and f" on each interval. For instance, the first interval at the far left will look like this:

This is the shape that corresponds to a negative f' and a positive f", and we found that f' is negative and f" positive on the interval (-∞,-4). We draw that graph segment so that it ends at the plotted point (-4,-225).

The graph segment connecting (-4,-225) with (-2.3, -111) must correspond to a positive f' and positive f", and so must look like this:

Continuing the process all the way to ∞, our final graph looks like this:

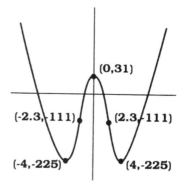

Observations on the graph in the preceding example:

1. The points (-2.3,-111) and (2.3,-111) mark the places where the graph changes its concavity from up to down or vice versa. To say the same thing in a different way, these are the points where f" changes its sign. Points at which the concavity of a graph switches are called *points of inflection.*

2. Note that the function f(x) = x⁴ - 32x² + 31 is an even function, because f(-x) = f(x) for all x. Therefore, the graph is symmetrical with respect to the y-axis. That means we could have drawn only the right-hand side of the graph using the calculus techniques, and then drawn the mirror image on the other side.

3. Although the problem did not explicitly ask for maxima and minima, we can see easily from the graph that f has absolute and relative minima at -4 and 4, a relative maximum at 0, and no absolute maximum. A correctly drawn graph should always enable us to identify and classify extrema.

Example:

Sketch the graph of f(x) = x - 2sin x.

Solution:

Since sin x is a periodic function and changes direction an infinite number of times over its domain, there are likely to be infinitely many interesting points. However, we can restrict our attention to the interval [-2π,2π], and assume that the graph we get will give us an accurate picture of the graph for the entire domain.

$$f'(x) = 1 - 2\cos x$$
$$f''(x) = 2\sin x$$

The zeros of f'(in our chosen interval) are: $-\frac{5\pi}{3}$, $-\frac{\pi}{3}$, $\frac{\pi}{3}$, and $\frac{5\pi}{3}$. .

The zeros for f"are: -2π, -π, 0, π, and 2π.

If we calculate the signs for in the appropriate intervals, and put the results together on a number line, we get:

101

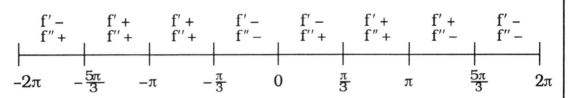

We then calculate the value of the original function f(x) at each interesting value, and plot the corresponding points. The points we get via this process are:

$$\left(-2\pi, -6.28\right),\ \left(-\frac{5\pi}{3}, -6.97\right),\ \left(-\pi, -3.14\right),\ \left(-\frac{\pi}{3}, 0.68\right),\ (0,0),\ \left(\frac{\pi}{3}, -0.68\right)$$
$$\left(\pi, 3.14\right),\ \left(\frac{5\pi}{3}, 6.97\right),\ \left(2\pi, 6.28\right)$$

Finally, we connect the plotted points with the graph segments shaped as called for by the signs of f′ and f″ as shown on the number line above.

From the graph of the intervals [-2π, 2π], which we have drawn, we can reasonably conclude that the graph of the same function on a wider interval looks something like this:

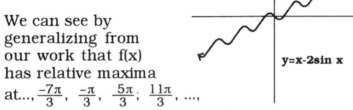

We can see by generalizing from our work that f(x) has relative maxima at..., $\frac{-7\pi}{3}$, $\frac{-\pi}{3}$, $\frac{5\pi}{3}$, $\frac{11\pi}{3}$, ..., relative minima at..., $\frac{-11\pi}{3}$, $\frac{-5\pi}{3}$, $\frac{\pi}{3}$, $\frac{7\pi}{3}$, ..., and points of inflection at..., -2π, -π, 0, π, 2π,...

Vertical Asymptotes

Recall that an **asymptote** for the graph of f(x) is a straight line which the graph of f(x) squeezes up against. Also remember that any vertical line in the xy-plane has an equation of the form x = c, where c is some number. Any function with a denominator will have a vertical asymptote at x = each zero of the denominator. The four pictures below illustrate the manner in which graph of f(x) can squeeze up against a vertical asymptote:

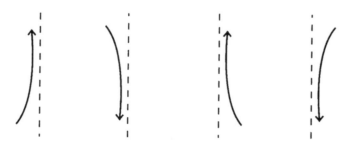

102

The signs of the first and second derivatives will inform us which of the illustrations applies to any particular case. For example, the first diagram above shows a graph which is increasing and concave up; that illustration will apply if the interval just to the left of the asymptote has positive first and second derivatives.

Since f(x) itself is undefined at any zero of its denominator, f' and f" will also be undefined at the same value; therefore a zero of the denominator of a function will always be an "interesting point", and will be one of the endpoints we use to divide our number line into intervals when testing the signs of f' and f".

Horizontal Asymptotes

The graph of f(x) has a horizontal asymptote if either $\lim_{x \to \infty} f(x)$ or $\lim_{x \to -\infty} f(x)$ are defined. The horizontal asymptote will be the line y = the limit. The horizontal asymptote has no relevance to the graph except at the far left and far right, as x approaches plus or minus infinity. The graph might cross the horizontal asymptote toward the "middle" of the graph, as many times as it pleases. At the left and right extremes, the graph will approach the horizontal asymptote in a manner similar to one of these four illustrations:

The procedure for graphing functions with asymptotes is similar to the procedure used for the last two examples, with several additions:

1. Identify the vertical asymptotes, if any, and draw them as dotted lines on the graph.

2. Identify the horizontal asymptote, if any, by calculating $\lim_{x \to \infty} f(x)$ or $\lim_{x \to -\infty} f(x)$. Draw the horizontal asymptote as a dotted line on the graph.

3. Proceed according to the same steps outlined for functions without asymptotes, remembering to squeeze against the vertical asymptotes in the intervals immediately adjacent to the asymptotes, and against the horizontal asymptote in the first and/or last interval, as x approaches plus or minus infinity. The signs of f' and f" will tell us the manner in which the "squeezing" is to be done.

Example:

Sketch the graph of f(x) = $\frac{e^x}{x-2}$.

103

Solution:

First we note that $\lim_{x \to -\infty} f(x) = 0$, so the graph will have y = 0 (i.e., the x-axis) as a horizontal asymptote as the graph goes off to the left. Since $\lim_{x \to \infty} f(x)$ is undefined, there is no horizontal asymptote on the right. Secondly, 2 is the only zero of the denominator; hence x = 2 is the sole vertical asymptote for this graph, and we draw a dotted line at x = 2 right away.

We calculate f′ and f″:

$$f'(x) = \frac{e^x(x-3)}{(x-2)^2}$$

$$f''(x) = \frac{e^x(x^2-6x+10)}{(x-2)^3} \quad \text{(after much work!)}$$

f′(x)=0 has only one solution; namely, x = 3. f″(x) = 0 has no solution, because e^x can never be zero no matter what x is, and the quadratic $x^2 - 6x + 10$ has no zeros, as can be seen by using the quadratic formula. Of course, f′ and f″ are undefined at x = 2, so 2 and 3 are our only interesting points. By testing the signs of both f′ and f″, we get the following number line:

The signs f′ and f″ on the interval (-∞,2) tell us that the graph is decreasing and concave down on the far left interval. This fact requires the graph to squeeze against the x-axis from below as x approaches negative infinity, and also requires the graph to plunge downward toward the vertical asymptote x = 2. Note that the only alternative, in both situations, would require the graph to be increasing concave up on the far left interval.

According to our number line, the graph is decreasing concave up on the interval (2,3), which means the graph must come down from above as it leaves the vertical asymptote at x = 2. Finally, on the interval (3,∞), the graph must be increasing, concave up as it heads off to the right. To get the y-coordinate of the point on the graph where x = 3, we calculate f(3) = 20 (approximately).

In short, we have only three intervals to draw in this graph, and only one point we need to plot exactly. The function has a relative minimum at x = 3, no maxima of any kind, and no inflection points.

104

Slant Asymptotes

The graph of f(x) sometimes approaches a non-horizontal straight line as x goes to plus or minus infinity. There are several cases in which this might happen, but the most common (and easiest to handle) is a rational function in which the numerator has degree one larger than the degree of the denominator. In the book **Straight Forward Pre-Calculus**, we learned that the equation of the slant asymptote in this case is y = (the quotient you get when you divide the denominator into the numerator and ignore the remainder). There is also another method, which uses calculus tools, for finding the slant asymptote.

The equation of a slant asymptote for the graph y = f(x) is:

$$y = mx + b$$

where:

$$m = \lim_{x \to \pm\infty} f'(x)$$

$$\text{and} \quad b = \lim_{x \to \pm\infty} (f(x) - mx).$$

The procedure for graphing functions which have slant asymptotes is identical to the procedure for graphing functions with horizontal asymptotes. The signs of the first and second derivatives in the far left and far right intervals will tell us the manner in which the graph will approach the slant asymptote.

NOTE: The graph of a rational function (and most other functions) will have at most one horizontal or slant asymptote. It will *not* have both.

Example:

Sketch the graph of $f(x) = \dfrac{2x^2 + 7x - 30}{x+2}$.

Solution:

Since the degree of the numerator (2) is one more than the degree of the denominator, this graph will have a slant asymptote. There is also a vertical asymptote at x = -2, which is the only zero of the denominator.

$$f'(x) = \frac{2x^2 + 8x + 44}{(x+2)^2}, \text{ and has no zeros,}$$

and $f''(x) = \dfrac{-72}{(x+2)^3}$, which also has no zeros

So the only interesting value is x = -2, where f' and f" are both undefined.

To find the equation of the slant asymptote, we take

$$m = \lim_{x \to \infty} f'(x) = \lim_{x \to \infty} \frac{2x^2 + 8x + 44}{(x+2)^2} = 2 \text{(by using L'Hopital's Rule)}.$$

$$\text{Then} \quad b = \lim_{x \to \infty} (f(x) - mx)$$

$$= \lim_{x \to \infty} \left(\frac{2x^2 + 7x - 30}{x+2} - 2x \right) = \lim_{x \to \infty} \left(\frac{3x-30}{x+2} \right)$$

$$= 3 \text{ (again by using l'Hopital's Rule)}.$$

So the slant asymptote is $y = 2x + 3$.

Our number line with the signs of looks like this:

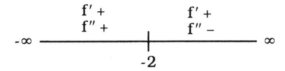

So the graph has just two segments: the first, increasing concave up, covers the interval $(-\infty, -2)$. The second, increasing concave down, covers the interval $(-2, \infty)$. The characteristics of those two segments also determine the manner in which the graph will squeeze up against the slant asymptote $y = 2x + 3$, and the vertical asymptote $x = -2$. Note that we don't really need to plot any specific points at all to get a reasonably accurate graph. However, it is easy to calculate $f(0) = -15$. Also, since the numerator factors, we can see that the zeros of the function are -6 and 2.5. So we can plot the points $(0, -15)$, $(-6, 0)$, and $(2.5, 0)$ for greater accuracy.

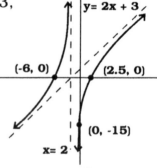

Note that the graph has no relative or absolute extrema, and no points of inflection.

Applications of Derivatives. Exercise 4. Curve Sketching.

Sketch each of the graphs. Label all asymptotes, maxima, minima, and points of inflection.

1. $y = x^6 - 16x^3$

2. $y = (x^2 - 16)(x^2 - 9)$

3. $y = \frac{1}{3}x^3 + \frac{1}{2}x^2 - 2x - 2$

4. $y = -\frac{2}{9}x^3 - \frac{2}{3}x^2 + \frac{16}{3}x + \frac{160}{9}$

5. $y = \frac{x^2 - 16x - 7}{x - 4}$

6. $y = \frac{x-1}{x^2 - 16}$

7. $y = \frac{x^2 - 9}{x^2 - 1}$

8. $y = \frac{x^2 - 1}{x^2 - 9}$

9. $y = \frac{3x^3 - x}{x^2 - 9}$

10. $y = (\cos x) - x$ on $[-2\pi, 2\pi]$

11. $y = 4x - \tan x$ on $[0, 4\pi]$

12. $y = (\ln x) - 3x$

Part 5

Differentials and Linear Approximations

Shown here is the graph of a function, along with the tangent line at a point on the graph. It is noticeable that the graph of the tangent line is very close to the graph of the function itself, for values of x close to the point where the tangent line is drawn. In fact, for a short interval the two graphs are almost indistinguishable from each other. This fact is of great help in *approximating* the value of the function for x-values close to the x-value where the tangent line is drawn. The function itself might be extremely complicated, but the equation of a tangent line always has the form y = mx + b for some numbers m and b. Calculating the y-coordinate of a point on the tangent line, when we are given the x value, is therefore a comparatively simple task.

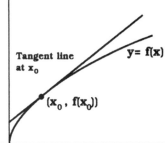

Example:

Estimate $\sqrt[3]{26.9}$.

Solution:

What we are asked for is the value of f(26.9), when f(x)= $\sqrt[3]{x}$.
We know that f(27) = 3, since 3 is the cube root of 27. Since 26.9 is close to 27, we can calculate the equation of the tangent line to y= $\sqrt[3]{x}$ at x = 27, and then figure out the y-coordinate of the point on that tangent line, where x = 26.9:

> By using the same procedure introduced in Chapter 2, we find
>
> $$f'(x) = \frac{1}{3\left(\sqrt[3]{x}\right)^2},$$
>
> $f'(27) = \frac{1}{27},$
> and f(27) = 3, so that the equation of the tangent line at x = 27 is
>
> $$y - 3 = \frac{1}{27}(x - 27)$$
> $$\text{or}$$
> $$y = \frac{1}{27}x + 2.$$

Substituting 26.9 into the equation of the tangent line, we get
y = 2.996296296, to 9 decimal places. The actual value of $\sqrt[3]{26.9}$, to the nearest 9 decimal places, is 2.996291714, so our estimate is good to within 5 decimal places after the decimal point. In fact,

---

even $\sqrt[3]{25.9}$ would have been estimated accurately to within three places after the decimal point by using this procedure. However, the farther we go from 27, the less accurate our estimate would become.

The example above is an instance of the use of a **differential**. Recall that the slope of any straight line can be thought of as "the difference in y, over the difference in x." In finding the equation of a tangent line, we always use the value of f'(x) as the slope, so we can say that

$$\frac{\text{difference in y}}{\text{difference in x}} = f'(x).$$

If we multiply both sides of that equation by "difference in x", we get:

"difference in y" = (f'(x))·"difference in x"

The technical terms for the phrases "difference in x" and "difference in y" on the tangent line are the **differential dx** and the **differential dy** respectively. Therefore the equation above can be written as:

dy = f'(x)·dx.

As long as we are talking about the tangent line, the equation above remains true for dx = (the difference in x-values between any two points on the tangent line), and dy = (the difference in y-values' between the same two points). Note that dy does <u>not</u> stand for the difference in y-values between two points on the graph of the <u>function</u>. That value, the difference in the values of the <u>function itself</u> at two different points is sometimes denoted Δy, or "delta y." The point of the procedure we used in the last example is that dy is sometimes a good approximation of Δy.

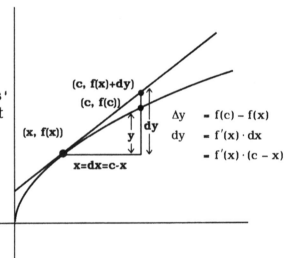

Using the language of differentials, we can describe the procedure this way:

Linear Approximations Using Differentials

Suppose we want the value of f(c) and that x_0 is a number near c such that $f(x_0)$ and $f'(x_0)$ are easy to calculate. We do the following:

1. Let dx = c - x_0.

2. Find $f'(x_0)$.

3. Let dy = $f'(x_0)$·dx.

4. Then f(c) is approximately $f(x_0)$ + dy.

In one simple formula : f(c) $\approx$ $f(x_0)$ + $f'(x_0)$(c - x_0).

Example:

Estimate sin 2°.

Solution:

The first thing we must do is to convert 2° to *radians*. Calculus simply doesn't work with trigonometric functions of degrees. Using the standard formula:

2 degrees = $\frac{2\pi}{180}$ (approximately .0349066) radians.

If $f(x) = \sin x$, then $f'(x) = \cos x$. We want $f\left(\frac{2\pi}{180}\right)$. Since $\frac{2\pi}{180}$ is close to 0, we can use $x_0 = 0$, and $c = \frac{2\pi}{180}$.

Since $f'(0) = \cos 0 = 1$, and $f(0) = \sin 0 = 0$, the formula above gives:

$$f\left(\frac{2\pi}{180}\right) \approx 0 + 1\left(\frac{2\pi}{180} - 0\right) = \frac{2\pi}{180}, \text{ or approximately } .0349066.$$

The actual value of the sine of 2° is .0348994967, which is very close.

Note that this example reveals a useful, more general fact: For small values of x, sin x (with x in radians) is approximately equal to x itself.

Another useful application of differentials is the estimating of errors. Suppose some quantity y depends upon some other quantity x according to a function $y = f(x)$, and suppose we have a measurement of x which is accurate to within some possible error dx. Then the possible error in y will be approximately dy, calculated exactly as in the problem above:

$$dy = f'(x) \cdot dx$$

Example:

Suppose one edge of a cube is known to be 14 cm long, to within 0.3 cm. Estimate the possible error in the volume of the cube.

Solution:

If we let x = the length of each edge, then the volume is related to x by the formula:
$$V = x^3.$$

Therefore, by our definition above, $dV = 3x^2 dx$. If we use x = 14 and dx = 0.3, we get:

$$dV = 3(14^2)(0.3) = 176.4 \text{ cm}^3.$$

Although the answer seems large, it is not too large as a proportion of the total volume of $14^3 = 2744 \text{ cm}^3$.

Applications of Derivatives. Exercise 5. Differentials and Linear Approximations.

In problems 1-6, use the methods described in this Part to estimate the function value.

1. $f(x) = \dfrac{1}{(6-x)^2}$; $f(5.11)$

2. $f(x) = x^4 + x^3 + x^2 + x + 1$; $f(0.92)$

3. $f(x) = 3^x - 2x$; $f(-0.1)$

4. $f(x) = \cos x$; $f(0.48\pi)$

5. $f(x) = \ln(x + 4)$; $f(-3.17)$

6. $f(x) = \sqrt[5]{x}$; $f(32.3)$

7. The shortest leg of a 30°–60°–90° triangle is measured as 6 light years, with a possible error of 0.04 light years. Estimate the error in the area of the triangle.

8. The radius of a circle is known to be 24 inches, plus or minus a quarter inch. Estimate the possible error in the area of the circle.

Part 6 | Newton's Method

If we knew how to find the zeros of any function in the world, we could solve any equation in the world. For example, the solution to the equation

$$3x^2 + \ln(5x) = e^{x-2} - 4\sec x$$

are just the zeros of the function

$$f(x) = 3x^2 + \ln(5x) - e^{x-2} + 4\sec x .$$

Needless to say, there is no formula for finding the zeros of a function such as the one above. There is a method, however, called **Newton's Method**, which enables us to get a very close approximation to a zero of a differentiable function if we can at least identify an x value which is close to a zero for the function. The procedure is a recursive procedure; that is, it is a procedure to be repeated again and again until we have our answer to a satisfactory degree of accuracy. The procedure is:

Newton's Method:

> Suppose f(x) is differentiable, and has a zero somewhere "fairly close" to x = c. Then:
> 1. Let $x_1 = c$.
> 2. Compute $x_2 = x_1 - \dfrac{f(x_1)}{f'(x_1)}$.
> 3. Compute $x_3 = x_2 - \dfrac{f(x_2)}{f'(x_2)}$.
> 4. Continue to compute $x_{n+1} = x_n - \dfrac{f(x_n)}{f'(x_n)}$
>   for each n, until $x_{n+1} = x_n$ to within as many decimal places as the degree of accuracy we want. x_n is then the answer we want.

Example:

Find a zero of $f(x) = \frac{1}{3}x^3 - x^2 - 8x + 39$, between -6 and -5.

Solution:

First, notice that f(-6) = -21 (negative), and f(-5) = 12.333...(positive). The Intermediate Value Theorem (See Chapter 1, Part 8), then tells us that there is a zero between -6 and -5. Having no further information, we might as well start the process with $c = x_1 = -5.5$.

We differentiate f(x) to get $f'(x) = x^2 - 2x - 8$. Our formula for each new x is:

$$x_{n+1} = x_n - \frac{\frac{1}{3}x_n^3 - x_n^2 - 8x_n + 39}{x_n^2 - 2x_n - 8} .$$

By substituting -5.5 for x_1, we get $x_2 = -5.418546366$.

Then substituting that number into the formula above to find x_3, we get x = -5.417212565.

Another repetition of the process yields $x_4 = -5.417212210$.

If we use that last value to calculate x_5, we will get -5.417212210 again, which means we have found the answer to within 9 digits beyond the decimal point.

We can check our answer by substituting -5.417212210 into the original f(x), and we will find that f(-5.41721220) = 0.

BIG-TIME WARNING

It does matter what we choose as our first estimate x_1. For example, if we had chosen $x_1 = -1$, that number would have been so far off that our successive approximations would have been:

$x_1 = -1$
$x_2 = 8.133333333$
$x_3 = 6.053199868$
$x_4 = 4.367945103$
$x_5 = -1.076268961$
$x_6 = 8.741427179.$

and it is obvious that our values for the x_n's are not getting any closer to an answer.

The idea behind the Newton Method is the same as the idea used in the previous part: The tangent line to y = f(x) is a close approximation to the graph of f(x) itself, for values of x which are close to the point at which the tangent line was drawn. x_2 is the x-intercept of the tangent line at x = -5.5. We then draw the tangent line to f(x) at x_2, and x_3 is the x-intercept of

that next tangent line. Here is a
magnified picture of what is happening:

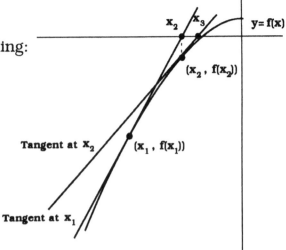

Finding a Zero from a Graph

A graph, produced by a graphing calculator or computer, can often give us an initial value to use for x to start Newton's Method.

Example:

The graph of $y = \frac{1}{4}x$ and $y = \ln x$, together on
the same axes, show two intersections,
where $\frac{1}{4}x = \ln x$. Find these two
intersections.

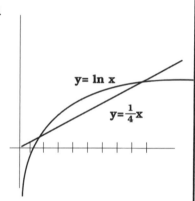

Solution:

The equation $\frac{1}{4}x = \ln x$ is equivalent to the
equation $\frac{1}{4}x - \ln x = 0$, so we are looking for
the zeros of the function:

$$f(x) = \frac{1}{4}x - \ln x.$$

The graph shows one intersection between 1 and 2, and another
between 8 and 9. So we use the Newton Method with $x_1 = 1.5$, and
then again with $x_1 = 8.5$.

Differentiating, we get $f'(x) = \frac{1}{4} - \frac{1}{x}$ so that the formula for Newton's
Method will be:

$$x_{n+1} = x_n - \frac{\frac{1}{4}x_n - \ln x_n}{\frac{1}{4} - \frac{1}{x_n}}$$

$$= x_n - \frac{x_n^2 - 4x_n \ln x_n}{x_n - 4} \ .$$

The approximations we get when we begin with x = 1.5 are:

x_1 = 1.5
x_2 = 1.426883741
x_3 = 1.429607776
x_4 = 1.429611825
x_5 = 1.429611825, etc.

Beginning with x = 8.5, we get:

x_1 = 8.5
x_2 = 8.613833235
x_3 = 8.613169479
x_4 = 8.613169456
x_5 = 8.613169456, etc.

So the two values for which $\frac{1}{4}x = \ln x$ are 1.429611825 and 8.613169456, to the nearest nine places after the decimal point.

Applications of Derivatives. Exercise 6. Newton's Method.

In problems 1-6, find a solution to the equation using the given value as the first approximation. Use at least 3 digits beyond the decimal point.

1. $x^4 - 7x^3 + 2x^2 + 5x - 21 = 0$; 7

2. $x^5 + 8x^4 - 12x^3 = 55$; -1

3. $2e^{-x} = \sin x$; 1

4. $\sqrt{3x^2 + 5x - 2} - 2x + 1 = 0$; 9

5. $0.2x^3 + 0.3x^2 + 0.4x + 0.5 = 0$; -2

6. $\ln x = x - 8$; 10

7. Let $f(x) = x^4 + x^3 + x^2 + x - 50$. Find a zero for f(x) by Newton's Method.
   Decide where to begin by calculating f(x) for each integer x from -5 to -1.

8. Let $f(x) = x^4 + x^3 + x^2 + x - 50$, as in Problem 7. Find out where f(x) has
   a relative extremum between -1 and 0.

Part 7

Optimization Problems-Part 1

An optimization problem is a word ("story") problem in which the object is to find out how to get the greatest, or the least, possible quantity in some real-world situation. We base many of our decisions on a desire to spend the least money or the least time, or to maximize our income or our grade point averages. If we can express the quantity we want to maximize as a function of some other variable, then we can use the ideas from Part 3 of this Chapter to find the point at which the maximum or minimum occurs.

The following is a sketch of the procedures to follow in solving optimization problems. Comments on the steps will follow afterwards.

1. Identify the unknown(s).

2. Identify the quantity to be maximized or minimized.

3. If the problem is a geometric problem, draw a diagram of the situation.

4. Assign a letter to each variable quantity in the problem, and write down explicitly what each letter stands for.

5. Write down a simple (or as simple as possible) equation for the quantity to be maximized or minimized (the quantity identified in Step 2), in terms of the variables identified in Step 4.

6. Use the information in the problem to construct an additional equation (or equations) which define(s) the relationships among the variables defined in Step 4.

7. Use the equation(s) from Step 6 to make substitutions into the Step 5 equation to get the right-hand side of that equation down to one variable. The Step 5 equation should now have the form $Q = f(x)$, where Q is the quantity to be maximized or minimized (from Step 2), and x is some other variable.

8. Determine the domain of the Step 7 function $f(x)$.

9. Find the absolute maximum or minimum for $f(x)$, subject to the domain identified in Step 8, as in Part 3.

10. Use the results of Step 9 to determine the answer—the value(s) of the unknown(s) identified in Step 1.

Comments on the steps in the procedure above:

1. This is the first step in *any* story problem. Sometimes there will be more than one unknown, such as the x- and y-coordinates of a point or the dimensions of a rectangle.

2. This quantity *might* be the same as the quantity in Step 1, but it might not! We will show examples of both situations later.

4. A failure to do and understand this step correctly is a primary reason that most people have trouble with story problems. Each

letter can mean one and only one thing, and each quantity in the problem should have one and only one letter assigned to it. For example, suppose we are dealing with a problem involving a trip from Chicago to Los Angeles, going through Denver. We can <u>not</u> just use the letter *t* to stand for *time*, because the problem contains 3 different times: the time from Chicago to Denver, the time from Denver to Los Angeles, and the total time from Chicago to Los Angeles (which is the total of the other two times, if there is no waiting time in Denver!). We must be able to identify <u>precisely</u> what each letter stands for! We will, of course, have to assign letters to the quantities identified in Steps 1 and 2, and probably to some other quantities as well. If the problem is a geometric problem for which we drew a diagram in Step 3, then we must assign a letter to each pertinent quantity in the diagram.

5. This step should not be complicated; it is not the step where the hard work is done. For example, if we are maximizing the area of a rectangle, we write down A = lw (where A stands for the area, l for the length, and w for the width.) Some books refer to this equation as the <u>objective equation</u>. When we get to the actual maximizing or minimizing step, the function we maximize or minimize will be a direct descendant of this equation. At this point, we might find that we did not label every quantity we need a letter for; in that case we go back to Step 4 and remedy the situation. In some cases, we might want to write the right-hand side of this equation in words rather than letters, so as not to complicate the situation with too many variables.

6. In simple problems, we will need to construct only one equation in this step. The problem will often have some constraint on the overall size of the situation, such as "We can spend up to $150", or "We have 540 square inches of cardboard to build a box with", etc. We can translate statements such as those into equations of the kind we are seeking in this step. This idea has caused some people to call the single equation in this step the <u>constraint equation</u>.

7. If we don't get enough from Step 6 to put our Step 5 equation in the form Q = f(x) with just one variable on the right-hand side, then we go back to Step 6 and try to construct some more equations. We might even have to bounce back and forth between Step 6 and 7 several times before we get it right. If the unknown (Step 1) is different from the quantity to be maximized or minimized (Step 2), then we want the one variable on the right-hand side to be unknown from Step 1 (or one of those unknowns, if more than one).

8. We decide the domain based on a common-sense interpretation of the problem. Frequently, for example, the meaning of the variable on the right-hand side is such that it would make no sense to have a negative value.

10. (We assume we are maximizing or minimizing Q = f(x).) If Q is also the unknown, then the answer to the problem is the value of f(x) at the maximum or minimum point. If x is the unknown, then the answer is the x value at the minimum or maximum point.

If there is another unknown in addition to x, the value of the other unknown should be easy to calculate from information in the problem or from equations used in Step 6.

Example:

Ben Dover wants to use 480 yards of fencing to create a fenced, rectangular area in his pasture. The fenced area will be divided into 6 smaller areas as shown in the diagram. What should be the dimensions of the entire fenced rectangle so that the total area of the fenced portion is the greatest possible?

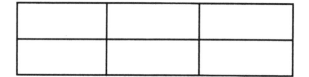

Solution:

Follow our steps:

1. The unknowns are the length and the width of the large fenced area.

2. The quantity to be maximized is the area of the large rectangle.

3. A diagram is already given.

4. We let A = the area of the large rectangle. We do NOT say simply, "A = area", because we also have six smaller areas in addition to the area of the large rectangle! Also, let x = the length of the large rectangle, and y = the width of the large rectangle, so that our diagram looks something like this when the dimensions are labeled:

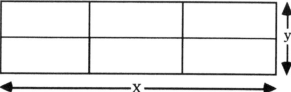

5. $A = xy$

6. The other information in the problem, which we have not yet used, is that the total amount of fencing will be 480 yards. If we can express that total in terms of x and y, we will have an equation that enables us to get rid of one of the two variables in the equation from Step 5. Looking at the diagram, we can see that the fencing will include 3 lengths (x), and 4 widths (y). Therefore, we have the equation:
$$3x + 4y = 480.$$

If we solve the above equation for y, we will get:

$$y = \frac{480 - 3x}{4} = 120 - \frac{3}{4}x.$$

7. We can now substitute $y = 120 - \frac{3}{4}x$ into the equation from Step 5, and we get:

$$A = x(120 - \frac{3}{4}x) = 120x - \frac{3}{4}x^2.$$

We now have a function of one variable, which we can maximize.

8. A negative length would make no sense. Also, since we have three lengths and only 480 total feet of fencing, the length (x) can't be more than 160 feet. So the domain of the function will be [0, 160].

9. The derivative of the function is $120 - \frac{3}{2}x$. Setting $120 - \frac{3}{2}x$ equal to zero and solving for x, we get x = 80. If we test the sign of the derivative on a number line, we get:

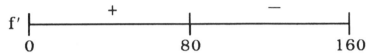

We can see from the number line that x = 80 will give us an absolute maximum for the function.

10. x was one of our unknowns, and we have already found that x = 80 for the maximum area. We have an equation from Step 6 which tells us that $y = 120 - \frac{3}{4}x$, and so we know

$$y = 120 - \frac{3}{4}(80) = 60.$$

The dimensions are therefore 80 yards by 60 yards.

Example:

Suppose we were given the exact same problem as in the Example above; but this time instead of asking for the dimensions, the problem states, "What is the largest possible area that Ben can fence off with his 480 yards of fencing?"

Solution:

The only steps in this solution which are different from the solution to the previous example are Steps 1 and 10. The answer to Step 1 is, "The area of the largest possible rectangle," in other words: A.

Since the unknown is the same as the quantity we are maximizing, Step 10 requires us to calculate the value of the function

$$f(x) = 120x - \frac{3}{4}x^2$$

when x = 80. Substituting x = 80 into f(x), we get A = 4800.
The largest possible area is 4800 square yards.

Example:

A toll road is to be built between Plopville and Gurgletown. A marketing study shows that if the toll is \$1.75, then 6500 vehicles per day will use the new road. However, if they reduce the toll, 100 additional vehicles will use the road (each day) for every cent the toll is reduced. What toll should be charged to maximize the daily revenue from the road?

Solution:

The unknown is the toll. The quantity to be maximized is the total revenue. The problem does not involve a diagram. The important quantities are:

R = total daily revenue
t = toll
n = number of vehicles using the road each day.

IMPORTANT NOTE: The "base" toll is given as \$1.75; in other words, in units of one dollar. However, the statement about the increase in vehicles says that there will be an increase of 100 for each cent decrease in the toll. Therefore, it is vital that we decide right now whether the letter t will stand for the toll in dollars or in cents! Either decision will work, but we must be consistent throughout the problem. Here we will assume that t stands for toll in cents. The reader is invited to do the problem with the toll expressed in dollars, and see that the answer comes out the same.

The simple equation that we want is R = tn, because the total money coming in is always the price (in this case, the toll) times the quantity (the number of vehicles).

The next step is the most complicated. We are told that the number of vehicles will be 6500 plus the number of additional vehicles which use the road because of a reduction in the toll. It can sometimes help in problems of this sort to assign a new letter, like a, to stand for the number of additional vehicles. So we have:

n = 6500 + a.

But we need to express a in terms of n and t, because we will eventually be substituting into the equation R = nt. The problem states that there will be 100 additional vehicles for each one-cent reduction for the base toll of 175 cents. If t stands for the new (reduced) toll, then the number of one-cent reductions from 175 cents is 175 - t. Therefore, the number of additional vehicles due to the toll reduction is:

a = 100(175 - t)
  = 17500 - 100t.

Now we can substitute a = 17500 - 100t into the equation n = 6500 + a, and we get:

n = 6500 + 17500 - 100t
  = 24000 - 100t.

We can then substitute 24000-100t for n in the equation R=tn, and get:

$$R = t (24000 - 100t)$$
$$= 24000t - 100t^2.$$

This is the function we will maximize. We certainly aren't going to make any money by charging a negative toll, so the domain of the function is $(0, \infty)$. The derivative of the function is $24000 - 200t$. When we solve for zero, we get $t = 120$. The number line showing the sign of the derivative is:

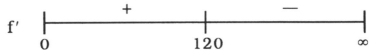

Therefore, $t = 120$ gives us the maximum revenue. Remember that t is being expressed in cents, so the more conventional answer is $t = \$1.20$.

Although the problem didn't ask what the maximum revenue was, we can calculate that simply by substituting $t = 120$ into the function $R = 24000t - 100t^2$, and the answer is 1,440,000 cents, or $14,400.00. Also, the number of vehicles when the toll is $1.20 will be $24,000 - 100t$, with t=120, which gives us $24,000 - 12,000 = 12,000$.

Applications of Derivatives. Exercise 7. Optimization Problems.

1. Neal Down wants to build a fenced-off area in his pasture with six subsections, the same arrangement as Ben Dover's in the earlier example (See page 116). The total area of the rectangle is 8112 square feet. What should be the dimensions of the entire area be if Neal wants to minimize the total length of all the fences?

2. Find two numbers whose product is 1681, such that the sum of the two numbers is as small as possible.

3. Find two numbers whose sum is 82, such that the product of the two numbers is as large as possible.

4. A rectangular box with a square base and no top is to be built with 2352 square inches of cardboard. What are the dimensions of the largest possible box (in volume)?

5. A rectangular box with no top and a height of 12 inches is to be made from 1728 square inches of material. What is the volume of the largest possible box?

6. A large, metal, cylindrical can is to have a volume of 3.456π cubic feet. Find the radius and height of the can which uses the smallest amount of metal. The volume (V) and total surface area (A) of a cylinder are given by the following formulas, where r = radius and h = height:

$$V = \pi r^2 h$$
$$A = 2\pi r(r + h)$$

7. Find the point (x- and y-coordinates) on the line $y = -2x - 3$ which is closest to the point (9, 4). (HINT: We can minimize the distance by minimizing the square of the distance).

8. We have a piece of wire $12+3\pi$ inches long. We want to cut the wire into two pieces, and make a square with one piece and a circle with the other. How should the wire be cut to maximize the total area of the circle and the square?

9. The U.S. Post Office has a limit on the size of packages it will accept for mailing. The length plus the girth (distance around the middle, as shown in the diagram) must be 84 inches or less. Find the dimensions of the rectangular package with a square end which will maximize the volume of the package.

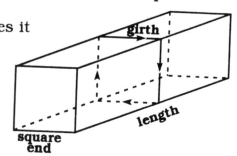

10. The cost of producing and selling x thousand widgets is $530x^2 - 18x^3 - 1226x + 1000$ dollars, and the income expected from selling x thousand widgets is $4810x - 135x^2$ dollars. For both of the given functions, we assume that $0 \le x \le 20$. How many widgets should be produced and sold in order to maximize the <u>profit</u>? (Note: profit = income - cost).

Part 8 — Optimization Problems-Part 2

The procedure for solving problems in this Part is the same as in the previous part. The only difference is that we will have to work harder to build the functions to be minimized or maximized. One possibility is:

Suppose we want to maximize or minimize the quantity Q, and we can easily express Q as a formula involving two variables, such as x and y. In the previous Part, we looked for information in the problem which enabled us to replace y with some expression involving x, so that our original formula could be written as a function of x only. However, sometimes we have to express both *x* and *y* as a function of some third variable, say *t*, and then express Q as a function of t.

Example:

Helen Hiwater is jogging westward along EZ Street. She is running toward the intersection with Fast Lane at 14 feet per second. Jerry Atrick is jogging toward that same intersection, going north on Fast Lane at 12 feet per second. Helen is 300 feet from the intersection at the exact same time that Jerry is 160 feet from the intersection. What is the closest the two runners will get to each ohter?

Solution:

The unknown in this case is the distance between the two joggers. That is also the quantity to be minimized. A diagram of the situation looks like this:

Using the Pythagorean Theorem, we can express the distance between Helen and

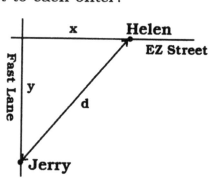

Jerry (which is both the unknown and the quantity to be minimized) in terms of x (Helen's distance from the intersection) and y (Jerry's distance from the intersection):

$$d^2 = x^2 + y^2$$

We can express both x and y in terms of the variable t, where t = the time (in seconds) elapsed since the point at which Helen is 300 feet from the intersection and Jerry is 160 feet from the intersection. Helen's distance from the intersection will be 300 feet, minus the distance covered in t seconds. Since Helen is jogging at 14 feet per second, she will have covered 14t feet in t seconds. This discussion leads to the equation:

$$x = 300 - 14t$$

Similar thinking gives:

$$y = 160 - 12t$$

We could use the two equations to express y in terms of x (or vice versa), but the resulting expression would be ugly. We decide instead to replace both x and y in the distance equation above, with expressions involving t:

$$d^2 = (300 - 14t)^2 + (160 - 12t)^2$$

Now, we remember that <u>we can minimize the distance by minimizing the square of the distance</u>. The idea is to avoid the messiness which would result from taking the square root of the right-hand side of the equation above. Our equation has only one variable on the right-hand side, so we can minimize the function

$$f(t) = (300 - 14t)^2 + (160 - 12t)^2.$$

Since both runners are heading toward the intersection at time t = 0, we know that their closest point will occur some time after t = 0. So we can assume that the domain of f is (0, ∞). The derivative is:

$$f'(t) = -28(300 - 14t) - 24(160 - 12t)$$
$$= 680t - 12240$$

Setting the derivative equal to zero, we get t = 18. The number line for the sign of f'(t) is:

So we can see that the minimum occurs at t = 18. The unknown, however, is the distance d. By substituting t = 18 into f(t), we get the square of the distance:

$$d^2 = f(18) = 5440.$$

To get the distance itself, we take the square root of 5440, which is approximately 73.76 feet, or about 73 feet 9 inches.

Sometimes the new variable to be used in the maximizing or minimizing function is even less obvious than in the previous example.

Example:

Two hallways, one 10 feet wide and the other 7 feet wide, intersect at right angles. How long is the longest ladder which can be carried horizontally around the corner?

Solution:

The unknown is the total length of the ladder, which is also the quantity to be maximized (actually that quantity will be *minimized* - see explanation below). It looks like this:

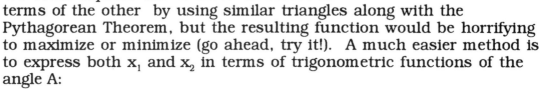

The total length of the ladder is $x_1 + x_2$. We could express one of those distances in terms of the other by using similar triangles along with the Pythagorean Theorem, but the resulting function would be horrifying to maximize or minimize (go ahead, try it!). A much easier method is to express both x_1 and x_2 in terms of trigonometric functions of the angle A:

We see from the diagram that $\cos A = \frac{7}{x_1}$, and that

$$\sin A = \frac{10}{x_2}.$$

Solving those equations for x_1 and x_2 , we get

$$x_1 = \frac{7}{\cos A}, \text{ and } x_2 = \frac{10}{\sin A}.$$

So the function of one variable which describes the length of the ladder is:

$$f(A) = \frac{7}{\cos A} + \frac{10}{\sin A} = 7(\cos A)^{-1} + 10(\sin A)^{-1}.$$

We will want the *minimum* value of this function on the domain $\left[0, \frac{\pi}{2}\right]$, because the ladder will have to be short enough to go around the corner at whatever point gives it the tightest fit from one wall to the other. Differentiating f(A), we get:

$$f'(A) = -7(\cos A)^{-2}(-\sin A) - 10(\sin A)^{-2}(\cos A)$$

$$= \frac{7\sin A}{\cos^2 A} - \frac{10\cos A}{\sin^2 A}$$

$$= \frac{7\sin^3 A - 10\cos^3 A}{\sin^2 A \cos^2 A}$$

Since a fraction is equal to zero only when the numerator is zero, we discard the denominator and set:

$$7\sin^3 A - 10\cos^3 A = 0$$

$$7\sin^3 A = 10\cos^3 A$$

$$7\frac{\sin^3 A}{\cos^3 A} = 10$$

$$7\tan^3 A = 10$$

$$\tan^3 A = 1.4286$$

$$\tan(A) = \sqrt[3]{1.4286}$$

Therefore, $A = \tan^{-1}\left(\sqrt[3]{1.4286}\right)$ = about 0.8447 (radians!).

Finally, we can find:

Total length = $x_1 + x_2$

$$= \frac{7}{\cos.8447} + \frac{10}{\sin.8447}$$

$$= 10.543 + 13.373$$

$$= 23.916 \text{ feet, or about 23 ft. 11 in.}$$

Applications of Derivatives. Exercise 8. Optimization Problems.

1. A Norman window in the shape of a semicircle on top of a rectangle is to have a total circumference of $36+9\pi$ (about 64.274) inches. Find the values of r and x which will maximize the total area of the window.

2. Suppose that, in Problem 1, the glass in the rectangular portion of the window admits twice as much light per square inch as the glass in the circular portion. Suppose that instead of maximizing the total area of the window, we want to maximize the total amount of light through the window. Once again, find the optimal values of r and x.

3. Suppose that, in Problem 1, there is a semicircle below the rectangle as well as one above the rectangle (the two semicircles have the same dimensions). Using the same total circumference as in Problem 1, find the values of r and x which will maximize the total area.

4. An eight-foot fence stands one foot away from a wall. Find the length of the shortest ladder which can reach the wall from outside the fence.

5. Sir Tifikit is on the bank of a river 144 yards wide. On the other side of the river, 756 yards downriver from his position, he sees the fair lady Emma Nemm being threatened by a dragon. Sir Tifikit

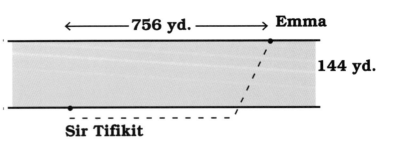

can run 8 yards per second, and he can swim 1.5 yards per second. How far down the bank should he run before he jumps into the water and swims to save Emma?

6. Paul Bearer is in an art museum, looking at a mural 3 feet high. The bottom of the mural is one foot above his eye level. How far away from the mural should Paul stand so that the angle of view filled by the mural is maximized? (HINT: the angle will be maximized if the tangent of the angle is maximized. Use the formula for the tangent of the difference of two angles.)

7. Metropolis is 10 miles from Liver River. Gotham City is 18 miles from the river on the opposite side from Metropolis, and 42 miles upriver. Ray Beeze plans to build a bridge across the river, with straight highways connecting the bridge to both Metropolis and Gotham City. At what point on the river should the bridge be built in order to minimize the total length of the two highways?

8. What is the area of the largest rectangle which can be circumscribed around an 11" x 15" rectangle in the manner shown?

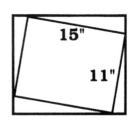

Part 9

Velocity and Acceleration

Suppose an object is moving along a straight line. We can treat the line like an x-axis, with a designated "zero point", and assign each point on the line a numeric value just like an x-coordinate. Points on one side of the zero point we be considered to have a negative value, and the points on the other side will have a positive value. Then, the position x of the object at time t can be expressed as a function of t:

$$x = x(t)$$

The <u>velocity</u> v of the object at time t is the rate at which the position of the object is changing; in other words:

$$v(t) = x'(t)$$

Acceleration (a), in turn, is the rate at which the velocity is changing. Therefore:

$$a(t) = v'(t)$$
$$= x''(t)$$

All three of these quantities (position, velocity, and acceleration) can be either positive or negative. The position is negative if the object is on the negative side of the zero point. The velocity is negative if the object is moving in the negative direction (usually left if the motion is horizontal, or down if the motion is up and down). The sign of the acceleration is a bit more complicated to explain:

> Acceleration is positive if the object is either moving in a positive direction and speeding up, or moving in a negative direction and slowing down.
>
> Acceleration is negative if the object is either moving in a negative direction and speeding up, or moving in a positive direction and slowing down.

Note: The <u>speed</u> of an object is the absolute value of the velocity. So the speed is always positive and ignores direction, while the velocity can be either positive or negative; the sign of the velocity reveals the direction of the motion.

Here are several more facts which help in solving velocity and acceleration problems:

> The object turns around (changes direction) whenever the sign of the velocity function changes.
>
> The object is speeding up when the velocity and acceleration have the same sign, and slowing down when the velocity and acceleration have opposite signs.

To find the total distance traveled in some time period, we have to determine the points at which the object turns around, calculate the distance traveled in each interval between the turnaround points, and then add those distances together.

Example:

A particle is moving along the x-axis according to the function:

$$x(t) = -4t^3 + 42t^2 - 120t + 95,$$

for $0 \leq t \leq 20$.

a. Determine the time intervals during which the particle is moving to the left.

b. Determine the values of t at which the particle changes direction, and find the position of the particle at each turnaround point.

c. Find the time intervals during which the particle is speeding up.

d. Find the farthest right and farthest left positions of the particle during the time $0 \leq t \leq 20$.

e. Find the total distance traveled by the particle in the time period $0 \leq t \leq 20$.

Solution:

We will need the functions for velocity and acceleration, and also the number lines which show the signs of the velocity and acceleration functions. Differentiating the position function, once for the velocity and again for the acceleration, we get:

$$v(t) = x'(t) = -12t^2 + 84t - 120$$

$$a(t) = v'(t) = -24t + 84$$

If we set $v(t) = 0$, the solutions are 2 and 5. (If there had been any solutions outside the interval (0,20), we would have ignored them.) The only solution to $a(t) = 0$ is $t = 3.5$. Testing the signs of $v(t)$ and $a(t)$ in the appropriate intervals, we come up with the following number lines:

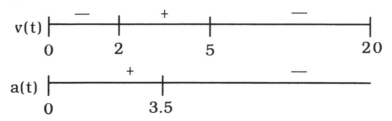

a. The number line for $v(t)$ shows that the velocity is negative in the intervals (0,2) and (5,20). Since negative velocity means motion toward the left, those two intervals are the answer to part a.

b. The particle changes direction when the velocity changes its sign. From the number line for v(t), we know that happens at t = 2 and t = 5. Substituting t = 2 and t = 5 into the position function x(t), we calculate x(2) = -9, and x(5) = 45.

c. The particle is speeding up when the acceleration and velocity have the same sign. We can see from the two number lines above that our answer is (2,3.5) and (5,20).

d. First, note that "find the farthest right and farthest left positions" is equivalent to "find the maximum and minimum values of the position function." By looking at the number line for v(t), or x'(t), we see that the candidates for the farthest right are x(0) and x(5). Since x(0) = 95 and x(5) = 45, the farthest point to the right in the path of the particle is x(0) = 95. The candidates for the farthest left position are x(2) = -9 and x(20) = -17505. Therefore the farthest left position is x(20) = -17505.

e. The number line for v(t) shows that we want to look at three intervals: [0,2], [2,5], and [5,20]. For each interval, we calculate the absolute value of the distance traveled by the particle (we don't care whether the particle was traveling leftward or rightward):

For $(0,2)$: $|x(2) - x(0)| = |-9 - 95| = 104$

For $(2,5)$: $|x(5) - x(2)| = |45 - (-9)| = 54$

For $(5,20)$: $|x(20) - x(5)| = |-17505 - 45| = 17550$
TOTAL: $104 + 54 + 17550 = 17708$

An important type of velocity and acceleration problem deals with objects which are thrown straight up or falling straight down. If gravity is the only force acting on such an object, and if we ignore the effect of air resistance, the position function for the object is:

$$x(t) = x_0 + v_0 t - 16t^2$$

Where x_0 = the initial position (height) of the object <u>in feet</u> (at time t = 0).
v_0 = the initial velocity of the object <u>in feet per second</u>—positive if the object is going upward, negative if downward.
t = time in seconds since the initial conditions.

Just as before, the velocity function is the derivative of the position function, so that

$$v(t) = v_0 - 32t$$

The second derivative of the position function is -32, which shows that the force of gravity (on the surface of Earth) causes objects to accelerate downward at 32 feet per second each second.

Things to remember in doing problems dealing with rising and falling objects:

1. The formulas above apply only so long as the object is moving

"freely" - no bounces or obstructions, no additional force such as a rocket engine.

2. An object is at ground level when x(t) = 0.

3. An object propelled upward reaches its maximum height when v(t) changes direction, which means when v(t) = 0.

4. When an object is "dropped", its initial velocity, v_0, is 0.

Example:

A ball is thrown upward from ground level with an initial velocity of 56 feet per second.
    a. How long does it take for the ball to hit the ground?
    b. How high does the ball go at its peak?

Solution:

We are given v_0 = 56 and x_0 = 0 (because we started at ground level). To do Part a, we want to know the value of t when x(t) = 0. We therefore solve the equation:

$$x(t) = 0 + 56t - 16t^2 = 0$$

The two solutions are t = 0 and t = 3.5. We already knew the ball was at ground level at t = 0, so the answer we want is t = 3.5.

For Part b, we want to know the value of x(t) when v(t) = 0. To get the answer, we first need to solve v(t) = 0 for t, and then substitute the answer for t in the function x(t):

$$0 = v(t) = 56 - 32t, \text{ so } t = 1.75$$
$$x(1.75) = 0 + 56(1.75) - 16(1.75^2) = 49.$$

So the ball rises to 49 feet before turning around and coming down.

Applications of Derivatives. Exercise 9. Velocity and Acceleration.

1. An object is moving along the x-axis according to the function
   $x(t) = \frac{1}{3}t^3 - 8t^2 + 48t + 10$, for t ≥ 0. Find all intervals during which the object is moving in a positive direction.

2. An object is moving along the x-axis according to the function $x(t) = \sin\frac{\pi t}{3}$, for 0 ≤ t ≤ 6. Find the intervals on which the object is speeding up.

3. An object is moving along the x-axis by the function x(t) = (t + 1) ln(.2t + .2) - t, with t ≥ 0.

    a. At what value(s) of t does the object change direction?

    b. How far does the object move between time t = 0 and the first time it changes direction?

4. Two particles are moving on a linear track according to the functions:

$$x_1 = t^2 + 2t$$

$$x_2 = -t^2 + 8t + 80$$

a. At what value of t will the two particles be in the same place?

b. Will they be going in the same or opposite directions at the point when they are in the same place?

c. At what value of t do the two particles have the same velocity?

d. Find all intervals on which the two particles are going in the same direction.

5. Phyllis Ophical drops a stone off a bridge. The stone hits the water 3.873 seconds later. How high is the bridge?

6. Luke Warm throws a stone off the same bridge as in Problem 5. The stone hits the water 3 seconds later. With what initial speed did Luke throw the stone?

7. A cantaloupe is projected straight up from the ground, and the satisfying SPLAT! is heard exactly 7.5 seconds thereafter. With what initial velocity was the cantaloupe projected?

8. Otto Biography drops a ball off a highway overpass (at a time when there is no traffic!). The ball bounces up from the highway with exactly half the speed with which it hit the pavement, and rises to a peak of 17 feet. How high is the overpass?

Part 10 — Related Rates

A "related rates" problem, in its simplest form, is a word problem in which two quantities (Q_1 and Q_2) have some permanent mathematical relationship, and Q_1 is changing at some given rate. The problem is to find the rate at which the second quantity, Q_2, is changing. The procedure for solving related rates problems is:

1. Identify Q_1 and Q_2. The unknown in the problem will be $\frac{dQ_2}{dt}$.

   $\frac{dQ_1}{dt}$ should be given in the problem.

2. Build an equation which describes the permanent relationship between Q_1 and Q_2. This equation should remain true throughout the changes in Q_2 and Q_1. Do not use instantaneous values, which are true at only one instant, in this step. The equation will not include $\frac{dQ_1}{dt}$ or $\frac{dQ_2}{dt}$ at this point.

3. Differentiate the equation from step #1 <u>with respect to t (time)</u>– this step is done similarly to the last example in Chapter 2 Part 12. After this step is done, the equation should include both $\frac{dQ_1}{dt}$ and $\frac{dQ_2}{dt}$.

4. Substitute the instantaneous values given in the problem, including $\frac{dQ_1}{dt}$, into the equation from step #3.

5. In some problems, the only unknown left will be $\frac{dQ_2}{dt}$.
   If there are any other unknown quantities in the equation at this point, use whatever information is available in the problem in order to get values for those quantities.

6. Solve for $\frac{dQ_2}{dt}$, which is the unknown.

Example:

A 15-foot ladder is leaning against a wall. The foot of the ladder is being pulled out at 8 inches ($\frac{2}{3}$ feet) per second. How fast is the top of the ladder falling when it (the top of the ladder) is exactly 12 feet high?

Solution:

The situation looks like this:

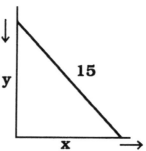

The quantity whose rate of change we know (i. e., Q_1), is x; the quantity whose rate of change we want (Q_2) is y. The permanent relationship between the two is given by the Pythagorean Theorem:

$$x^2 + y^2 = 15^2 = 225$$

Note that we do not use y = 12 at this stage, because y is not permanently equal to 12 throughout the change process. If we differentiate both sides of the equation with respect to t, we get:

$$2x\frac{dx}{dt} + 2y\frac{dy}{dt} = 0.$$

We are given y = 12, and $\frac{dx}{dt} = \frac{2}{3}$. We also need to find a value for x before we can solve for $\frac{dy}{dt}$. The original equation, $x^2 + y^2 = 225$, can be used with y = 12 to give us x = 9. Now our equation is:

$$18\left(\frac{2}{3}\right) + 24\frac{dy}{dt} = 0.$$

Solving for $\frac{dy}{dt}$, we find $\frac{dy}{dt} = -\frac{1}{2}$, which is our answer. The answer is negative because the top of the ladder is moving down, which means that the value of y is <u>decreasing</u>.

Example:

> A jet is flying 8 miles high at 720 mph. A searchlight, positioned
> directly under the path of the jet, is trained on the jet. How fast is
> the angle between the searchlight and the horizontal changing at
> the point when the jet passes directly overhead?

Solution:

A diagram of the situation is shown. We will set up
our equation using the angle A rather than B, because
the angle will be expressed in terms of its tangent.
When the jet is directly overhead, x will be 0, and the
tangent of angle B will not exist at that point. Since
angle B will decrease at the same rate as angle A increases,
we can get our answer just as easily by using angle A.

The quantity whose rate of change is given is x; the quantity whose
rate of change we want is angle A. The equation which gives the
relationship between x and A is:

$$\tan A = \frac{x}{8} = \frac{1}{8}x$$

Differentiating both sides with respect to t, we get:

$$\sec^2 A \frac{dA}{dt} = \frac{1}{8}\frac{dx}{dt}$$

When the jet is directly overhead, x and angle A are both equal to 0.
Since sec 0 = 1, our equation is now:

$$\frac{dA}{dt} = \frac{1}{8}\frac{dx}{dt}$$

The speed of 720 mph translates into $\frac{dx}{dt}$ = -720, since x is
decreasing. Substituting $\frac{dx}{dt}$ = -720, we can solve the above equation
for $\frac{dA}{dt}$, and we get -90 (radians per hour, since the angle is measured
in radians and the speed in miles per hour). Angle B, which is
actually the angle asked about in the problem, is therefore increasing
at 90 radians per hour. A more convenient measure would be degrees
per second. The reader is invited to verify that 90 radians per hour
translates into about 1.432 degrees per second.

Sometimes the rate at which the first quantity is changing is not given to us
directly, but can be calculated from given information.

Example:

> A ball is dropped from a 96-foot high platform. Hugh R. Yew is
> standing 40 feet away from the platform, watching the ball drop.
> How fast is the angle of his line of sight changing when the ball is
> halfway to the ground?

Solution:

A diagram of the situation is shown.

We want the rate $\frac{dA}{dt}$; we will be able to calculate the value of $\frac{dx}{dt}$. Therefore we want an equation which defines the relationship between x and angle A. The obvious equation is:

$$\tan A = \frac{x}{40} = \frac{1}{40}x.$$

If we differentiate both sides with respect to t, we get:

$$\sec^2 A \frac{dA}{dt} = \frac{1}{40}\frac{dx}{dt}.$$

In order to get a value for $\frac{dx}{dt}$, we get the value of t when the ball is halfway down. Then we use that value to find the velocity (which is the same thing as $\frac{dx}{dt}$) at that same time. For this, we use the formulas given in the previous part. We have $x_0 = 96$, $v_0 = 0$, and we want to find t and v when x = 48:

$$48 = x = 96 - 16t^2$$

Solving for t, we get $t = \sqrt{3}$. We then substitute $t = \sqrt{3}$ into the velocity formula:

$$\frac{dx}{dt} = v = -32t = -32\sqrt{3}$$

Remember we want to solve the equation

$$\sec^2 A \frac{dA}{dt} = \frac{1}{40}\frac{dx}{dt}$$

for $\frac{dA}{dt}$, which means we need values for $\frac{dx}{dt}$ and $\sec^2 A$. We calculated $\frac{dx}{dt} = -32\sqrt{3}$ above. From the Pythagorean Theorem, we can calculate $z = \sqrt{3904} = 8\sqrt{61}$. Therefore, $\sec^2 A = \left(\frac{\sqrt{3904}}{40}\right)^2 = 2.44$. Finally, we can substitute $\sec^2 A = 2.44$, and $\frac{dx}{dt} = -32\sqrt{3}$ into our equation, and get $2.44\frac{dA}{dt} = \frac{1}{40}\left(-32\sqrt{3}\right)$.

The solution is $\frac{dA}{dt}$ = -0.56789 (radians per second).

A related rates problem is sometimes complicated by the presence of two (or more) quantities whose rates of change are given, when the quantity whose rate of change is unknown is related to both of the first two quantities.

Example:

> A cylinder is changing shape such that its radius is decreasing by .5 inches per second, and its height is increasing by 1 inch per second. At what rate is the volume changing when the height is 8 inches and the radius 3 inches?
>
> Solution:
>
> The formula for the volume of a cylinder is: $V = \pi r^2 h$.
>
> Differentiating with respect to t, and realizing that V, r, and h are all functions of t, we get:
>
> $$\frac{dV}{dt} = 2\pi r h \frac{dr}{dt} + \pi r^2 \frac{dh}{dt}$$
>
> (we needed the product rule for the right-hand side).
>
> Now we can substitute r = 3, h = 8, $\frac{dh}{dt} = 1$, and $\frac{dr}{dt} = -.5$, giving us:
>
> $$\frac{dV}{dt} = 2\pi(3)(8)(-.5) + \pi(9)(1)$$
>
> Solving for $\frac{dV}{dt}$, we find that the volume is decreasing at 15π cubic inches per second.

Applications of Derivatives. Exercise 10. Related Rates.

1. The diameter of a circle is expanding at a rate of 2 feet per minute. How fast is the area of the circle expanding when the diameter is 6 feet?

2. The diameter of a sphere is increasing at 2 feet per minute. How fast is the volume of the sphere increasing when the volume = 420 cubic feet? $(V = \frac{4}{3}\pi r^3)$

3. Ray Needay is 6 feet tall, and he is walking away from a 24-foot tall lamp post at 4 feet per second. How fast is Ray's shadow lengthening when his distance from the lamp post is $\frac{\sqrt{5e}}{\pi}$?

4. Helen Hiwater is jogging westward along EZ Street, running toward the intersection with Fast Lane at 14 feet per second. Jerry Atrick is jogging toward that same intersection, going north on Fast Lane at 12 feet per second. Helen is 300 feet from the intersection, and Jerry is 160 feet from the intersection. How fast is the distance between the two runners decreasing? (This is the same situation as described in the first example in Part 8.)

5. A particle is moving along the graph of $y = x^2 + 4x - 12$ at a rate such that $\frac{dx}{dt} = -2.5$ units per minute. How fast is the y-coordinate changing when x = 4?

6. Under the same circumstance as Problem 5, how fast is the particle moving toward or away from the origin at the same time (x = 4)?

7. Two cars are on a collision course toward point P. The paths of the two cars make a 30 degree angle with each other. The first car is 40 km from P, and traveling toward P at 16 km/hour. The second car is 50 km from P, traveling at 20 km/hour. How fast is the (straight line) distance between the two cars decreasing? (HINT: Law of Cosines.)

8. A particle is moving along the line y = 6 in such a way that the x-coordinate is the following function of time:
$$x(t) = t^3 - 18t^2 + 92t - 120.$$

How fast is the distance between the particle and the origin changing when t = 4?

Part 11 **Mean Value Theorem**

The Mean Value Theorem is an important mathematical fact which is used in proving many more advanced theorems, although there are not many practical problems which use the theorem directly. The theorem is usually introduced by beginning with a simpler result, called Rolle's Theorem.

Rolle's Theorem

> Suppose:
>
> f(x) has the same value for two different numbers a and b (in other words, f(a) = f(b)),
>
> f is continuous on the closed interval $[a,b]$, and
>
> f'(x) exists everywhere between a and b.
>
> THEN there is some number c, between a and b, such that f'(c) = 0.

Geometrically, Rolle's Theorem says that if the graph of f(x) goes through two different points with the same y-coordinate (which means the two points lie on the same horizontal line), then the graph has a horizontal tangent somewhere in between the two points:

The proof of Rolle's Theorem, which can be found in most standard calculus texts, is based on the idea that there must be a local minimum or local maximum for f(x) on the closed interval $[a,b]$ (see Chapter 1, Part 8). By a theorem discussed in Part 3, f'(x) must be 0 for that maximum or minimum.

Examples:

1. If $f(x) = x^3 + 4x^2 - 25x + 64$, then $f(-4) = f(5) = 164$. Since $f(x)$ is a polynomial, it is continuous and differentiable everywhere. Therefore there is some number c between -4 and 5 for which $f'(c) = 0$. We can find the number c easily enough by setting $f'(x)$, which is $3x^2 + 8x - 25$, equal to zero and solving for x. The quadratic formula says that one of the answers is approximately 1.8465, which is between -4 and 5.

2. If $f(x) = \frac{x}{x^2-16}$, then $f(5) = f\left(\frac{-16}{5}\right) = \frac{5}{9}$. However, $f(x)$ is not continuous on the entire interval from $-\frac{16}{5}$ to 5; in particular, there is a discontinuity at x = 4. So Rolle's Theorem is no guarantee that there is a horizontal tangent between $-\frac{16}{5}$ and 5 (and in fact there isn't one).

Mean Value Theroem

Suppose:

f is continuous on the closed interval $[a, b]$, and

$f'(x)$ exists everywhere between a and b.

THEN there is some number c, between a and b, such that:

$$f'(c) = \frac{f(b)-f(a)}{b-a}$$

The expression which $f'(c)$ is supposed to be equal to, is actually the slope of the secant line between the two points (a, f(a)) and (b, f(b)). So the geometric interpretation of the Mean Value Theorem is: there is a point between a and b where the tangent line is parallel to the secant line between (a, f(a)) and (b, f(b)).

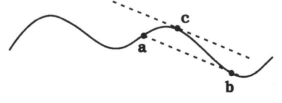

The picture makes it easy to see why the Mean Value Theorem is related to Rolle's Theorem. If f(a) = f(b), then the secant line between (a, f(a)) and (b, f(b)) is horizontal. In that case, the Mean Value Theorem and Rolle's Theorem both say the same thing.

Examples:

1. If f(x) = ln x, then f(2) = 0.69315 and f(3) = 1.09861. Therefore, the slope of the secant line between (2, f(2)) and (3, f(3)) is:

$$\frac{f(b)-f(a)}{b-a} = \frac{1.09861-0.69315}{3-2} = .40546$$

Since $f'(x) = \frac{1}{x}$, we can find the value 'c' which makes the Mean Value Theorem work by setting $\frac{1}{x} = .40546$.

The answer is 2.4663, which is between 2 and 3 as required.

2. If $f(x) = x^{\frac{2}{3}}$, then f(-1) = 1 and f(3.375) = 2.25. If the Mean Value Theorem applies, then there must be a value c, between -1 and 3.375, for which
$$f'(c) = \frac{2.25-1}{3.375-(-1)} = .2857.$$

However, $f'(x) = \frac{2}{3x^{\frac{1}{3}}}$, and the only solution to $\frac{2}{3x^{\frac{1}{3}}} = .2857$ is x = 12.7. 12.7 is not between -1 and 3.375. The Mean Value Theorem does not exist at x = 0 (which is part of the interval [-1, 3.375]).

Applications of Derivatives. Exercise 11. Mean Value Theorem.

In problems 1-3, f(a) and f(b) are both 0. In each case, either find a value of c, between a and b, for which f'(c) = 0, or explain why such a value c does not not exist.

1. f(x) = sin x; a = 0, b = 8π

2. f(x) = tan x; a = 0, b = π

3. f(x) = ln(x²); a = -1, b = 1

4. Use Rolle's Theorem to explain why -1 is the only zero of the function x³ + 3x² + 9x + 7.

In problems 5-7, either find a value c between a and b, for which $f'(x) = \frac{f(b)-f(a)}{b-a}$, or else explain why such a value does not exist.

5. $f(x) = \sin x$; $a = 0$, $b = \frac{3\pi}{4}$

6. $f(x) = |x + 2|$; $a = -1$, $b = 5$

7. $f(x) = e^x$; $a = 0$, $b = \ln 4$

8. The line $y = x + 5$ intersects the parabola $y = x^2 + x + 1$ twice. According to the Mean Value Theorem, this means there is a point on the parabola, between the two points of intersection, at which the tangent line is parallel to $y = x + 5$. Find the point and the equation of the tangent line.

Answers

Limits & Continuity. Exercise 1. Page 3-4.

1. $f: [-\frac{5}{2}, \infty)$

g: all real numbers except $-\frac{7}{2}$ and 6.

k: all real numbers.

j: all real numbers except $-\frac{3}{2}$.

2. f: $(-\infty, 3]$

k: all real numbers

3. $\frac{14x^2 + 16x - 14}{2x + 3}$

4. $\frac{(3x-2)(2x^2 - 5x - 42)}{(2x+3)(\ -x)}$

5. $\left(3 - \sqrt{2x+5}\right)\left(\frac{4-x}{2x^2 - 5x - 42}\right)$

6. $\frac{21x - 14}{14x - 5}$

7. $\frac{13x - 26}{2x + 3}$

8. $\frac{-35x - 14}{14x + 3}$

9. $\frac{13x - 26}{2x + 3}$

10. $\frac{21x - 98}{2x - 5}$

11. $3 - \sqrt{2(x+h) + 5}$

12. $\frac{3x+2}{3-2x}$ or $\frac{-3x-2}{2x-3}$

13. f : 2

g : 4

k : $\frac{4}{7}$

j : $\frac{2}{3}$

14. f : $3 - \sqrt{5}$

g : $-\frac{2}{21}$

k : -4

j : $-\frac{2}{3}$

15. f : 2

g : 4

k : $\frac{4}{7}$

j : $\frac{2}{3}$

16. $\frac{13}{4x^2 + 12x + 4hx + 6h + 9}$

17. (a) even (b) even and odd.
(c) odd (d) neither

18 a.

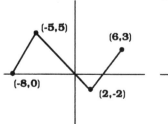

18 b.

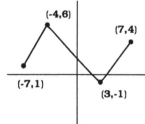

18 c.

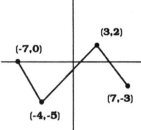

18 d.

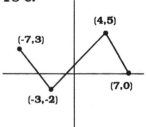

18 e.

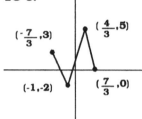

18 f.

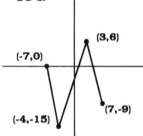

18 g.

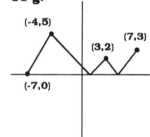

18 h.

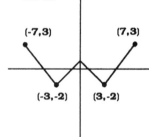

18 i.

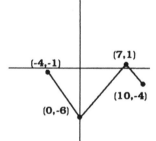

Limits & Continuity. Exercise 2. Page 7.

1. 10 **2.** 3 **3.** 2
4. 5 **5.** 4 **6.** 4

7. $\lim_{x \to 1} h(x) = 4; \ h(1) = \sqrt{\pi}$

8. -4 **9.** 2 **10.** -3

138

Limits & Continuity. Exercise 3. Page 10-11.

1. $\lim\limits_{x\to 2^-} f(x) = 1$

$\lim\limits_{x\to 2^+} f(x) = 1$

$\lim\limits_{x\to 2} f(x) = 1$

2. $\lim\limits_{x\to 2^-} f(x) = 1$

$\lim\limits_{x\to 2^+} f(x) = 1$

$\lim\limits_{x\to 2} f(x) = 1$

3. $\lim\limits_{x\to 2^-} f(x) = 1$

$\lim\limits_{x\to 2^+} f(x) = 1$

$\lim\limits_{x\to 2} f(x) = 1$

4. $\lim\limits_{x\to 2^-} f(x) = 1$

$\lim\limits_{x\to 2^+} f(x) = 3$

$\lim\limits_{x\to 2} f(x)$ is undefined.

5. $\lim\limits_{x\to 2^-} f(x) = 4$

$\lim\limits_{x\to 2^+} f(x) = 4$

$\lim\limits_{x\to 2} f(x) = 4$

6. $\lim\limits_{x\to 2^-} f(x) = 5$

$\lim\limits_{x\to 2^+} f(x) = 6$

$\lim\limits_{x\to 2} f(x)$ is undefined.

7. $\lim\limits_{x\to 2^-} f(x) = 5$

$\lim\limits_{x\to 2^+} f(x) = 6$

$\lim\limits_{x\to 2} f(x)$ is undefined.

8. $\lim\limits_{x\to 2^-} f(x) = 5$

$\lim\limits_{x\to 2^+} f(x) = 6$

$\lim\limits_{x\to 2} f(x)$ is undefined.

9. $\lim\limits_{x\to -4^-} f(x) = 4$

$\lim\limits_{x\to -4^+} f(x) = 4$

$\lim\limits_{x\to -4} f(x) = 4$

10. $\lim\limits_{x\to -4^-} f(x) = 4$

$\lim\limits_{x\to -4^+} f(x) = -3$

$\lim\limits_{x\to -4} f(x)$ is undefined.

11. $\lim\limits_{x\to -4^-} f(x) = -2$

$\lim\limits_{x\to -4^+} f(x) = -2$

$\lim\limits_{x\to -4} f(x) = -2.$

12. $\lim\limits_{x\to -4^-} f(x) = 4$

$\lim\limits_{x\to -4^+} f(x) = -3$

$\lim\limits_{x\to -4} f(x)$ is undefined.

Limits & Continuity. Exercise 4. Page 14.

1. -2   **2.** -2   **3.** 2

4. -2   **5.** 0   **6.** undefined

7. -2   **8.** $\frac{3}{2}$

Limits & Continuity. Exercise 5. Page 16.

1. undefined (b or c)   **2.** undefined (a)

3. undefined (c)   **4.** 0.9

5. $\frac{1}{\sqrt{2}}$ **6.** 2.6

7. undefined (b)   **8.** undefined (a)

9. undefined (d)   **10.** undefined (a)

11. undefined (c)   **12.** 0

13. undefined (d)   **14.** undefined (b)

Limits & Continuity. Exercise 6. Page 20-21.

1. (c) right continuous   **2.** (d) not continuous

3. (d) not continuous   **4.** (c) right continuous

5. (d) not continuous   **6.** (a) continuous

7. (b) left continuous   **8.** (d) not continuous

9. (d) not continuous   **10.** (b) left continuous

11. (d) not condinuous   **12.** (b) left continuous

13. (d) not continuous   **14.** (a) continuous

15. (c) right continuous   **16.** (d) not continuous

17. $(-\infty, -4], (0, \infty)$ **18.** $(-\infty, -4), (-4, 3), [3, \infty)$

19. $(-\infty\,-4), [0, 3), (3, \infty)$ **20.** $(-\infty, -4), [0, \infty)$

Limits & Continuity. Exercise 7. Page 22-23.

1. 0   **2.** $\frac{1}{3}$

3. undefined   **4.** 0

5. 3   **6.** 2

7. $-\frac{1}{3}$ **8.** 0

9. 0   **10.** undefined

11. 0   **12.** undefined

13. undefined   **14.** 1

15. $-\frac{1}{4}$ **16.** undefined

Limits & Continuity. Exercise 8. Page 27.

1. -4.39   **2.** -2.66

3. 2.71   **4.** 2.52

5. 10.34   **6.** 1.50

7. (-4, -3)   **8.** (0, 1)

9. (2, 3)   **10.** (-1, 0), (2, 3) or (4, 5)

11. (0, 1)   **12.** (-2, -1)

Derivatives. Exercise 1. Page 32.

1. -3   **2.** 0

3. Undefined (as x approaches -3 from below the slope is -1; as x approaches -3 from above, the slope is 1).

4. 0   **5.** 5

6. -4   **7.** y+8=x or y=x-8

8. y+6=3(x+1) or y=3x-3

9. y-7=x-4 or y=x+3

10. y=-(x=π) or y=π-x

11. y-2=2(x-ln2) or y=2x+2-2ln2 or

y=2x+.6137 (approx.)

12. y-3=-(x-3) or y=6-x

13. At (-2,-4), slope =-2

At (0,-6), slope =0

At (2,-4), slope =2

At (5,6.5), slope = 5

At (10,44), slope = 10

Slope of $y = \frac{1}{2}x^2 - 6$ at any point on the graph is the x-coordinate of the point.

14. At (ln(0.5), 0.5), slope =0.5

At (ln3,3), slope =3

At (ln6,6), slope =6

At (ln10,10), slope =10

The slope of $y=e^x$ at any point (x,e^x) is e^x, or the y-coordinate of the point.

Derivatives. Exercise 2. Page 38.

1. 3

2. - 4x

3. 3 - 4x

4. $\dfrac{-6}{(5+3x)^2}$

5. $\dfrac{-41}{(5+3x)^2}$

6. $3(x-1)^2$ or $3x^2 - 6x + 3$

7. $\dfrac{3}{2\sqrt{5+3x}}$

8. $\dfrac{x}{\sqrt{x^2-2}}$

9. - 20

10. $\dfrac{-3}{20}$

11. 27

12. $\dfrac{2}{3}$

13. - 5

14. $-\dfrac{1}{2}$

15. $-\dfrac{5}{8}$

16. $-\dfrac{3}{2}$

17. 8x - 12

18. $\dfrac{8}{(s+3)^2}$

Derivatives. Exercise 3. Page 41-42.

1. $20x^3 - 12x^2 + 2x$

2. $-5 + \dfrac{1}{2\sqrt{x}}$

3. $-5 + \dfrac{\sqrt{2}}{2\sqrt{x}}$

4. $\dfrac{-5}{4\sqrt{x^3}} + \dfrac{15}{x^6} + \dfrac{49}{8x^{\frac{1}{8}}} - 12$

5. 21

6. 39

7. $-\dfrac{363}{40}$ or - 9.075

8. $-\dfrac{363}{40}$ or - 9.075

9. 1

10. 4

11. $-\dfrac{47}{4}$ or - 11.75

12. $\dfrac{2303}{32}$ or 71.96875

13. $20t^4 - \dfrac{4}{5}t^{-\frac{4}{5}}$

14. $3t^2 - 2t - 5$

15. $-\dfrac{20}{t^6} + 12t^2 - 6$

16. $\dfrac{5}{2\sqrt{t}} - 6 + 36t^2$

17. y = 5x - 12

18. y = 5x - 12

19. y = 5x - 12

20. y = 5x - 12

21. (6, - 7)

22. (-4, 14), $(\frac{4}{3}, -\frac{1670}{27})$

23. (-3, - 64), (0, 71), (1, 64)

24. No points have horizontal tangents.

Derivatives. Exercise 4. Page 48-49.

1. $(6x-4)(\dfrac{3}{5\sqrt{x}} - 2x^7 + 2x) +$
$(\dfrac{-3}{10\sqrt{x^3}} - 14x^6 + 2)(3x^2 - 4x - 6)$

2. $\dfrac{10}{(7-6x)^2}$

3. $(6x-2)(-4x^3 + 5x^4 - 6x^5) +$
$(-12x^2 + 20x^3 - 30x^4)(1 - 2x + 3x^{2)}$

4. $\dfrac{48x^5 - 4x^3 + 12x^2}{(2x+1)^2}$

5. $\dfrac{73124}{9}$

6. $\dfrac{73}{6}$

7. $\dfrac{1519}{2888}$

8. $\dfrac{635}{24}$

9. - 5

10. - 54

11. 38

12. 24

13. $y = -\dfrac{9}{2}x - 4$

14. No tangent; derivative is undefined at x = 0.

15. y = -170x + 120

16. y = 11x - 2

17. No solution.

18. $(2, -\frac{1}{4}), (4, -\frac{1}{8})$

Derivatives. Exercise 5. Page 51.

1. 3, 0, 0.

2. 6x + 2, 6, 0, 0.

3. $15x^4 - 4x + 2$, $60x^3 - 4$, $180x^2$, $360x$, 360, 0, 0.

4. $p^{(n)}(x) = 0$ if and only if n is greater than the degree of p(x).

5. $\dfrac{172}{(2x+5)^3}$

6. - 108

7. No solution. Note : f(x) is undefined at $x = \dfrac{3}{2}$; therefore all derivatives of f(x) are also undefined at $\dfrac{3}{2}$.

8. e^x

Derivatives. Exercise 6. Page 57-58.

1. b　　　**2.** d　　　**3.** f

4. a　　　**5.** c　　　**6.** e

7. b　　　**8.** d　　　**9.** c

10. a　　**11.** b　　**12.** c

13. $(-\infty, -3)$ increasing, concave down.
$(-3, -1)$ decreasing, concave down.
$(-1, 1)$ decreasing, concave up.
$(1, -\infty)$ increasing, concave up.

14. $(-\infty, 1)$ decreasing, concave up.
$(1, 2)$ increasing, concave up.
$(2, 3)$ increasing, concave down.
$(3, \infty)$ decreasing, concave down.

15. $(-\infty, -2)$ decreasing, concave up.
$(-2, \dfrac{4-2\sqrt{13}}{3})$ increasing, concave up.
$(\dfrac{4-2\sqrt{13}}{3}, 0)$ increasing, concave down.
$(0, \dfrac{4+2\sqrt{13}}{3})$ decreasing, concave down.
$(\dfrac{4+2\sqrt{13}}{3}, 6)$ decreasing, concave up.
$(6, \infty)$ increasing, concave up.

16. $(-\infty, -1)$ decreasing, concave down.
$(-1, 0)$ decreasing, concave up.
$(0, 1)$ increasing, concave up.
$(1, \infty)$ increasing, concave down.

Derivatives. Exercise 7. Page 60-61.

1. $\dfrac{\sin x}{\cos^2 x}$, or tanx secx

2. $\dfrac{-\cos x}{\sin^2 x}$, or - cotx cscx

3. $\dfrac{-\sec^2 x}{\tan^2 x}$, or $-\csc^2 x$

4. $-\dfrac{3\pi}{2}$, $-\dfrac{\pi}{2}$, $\dfrac{\pi}{2}$, $\dfrac{3\pi}{2}$

5. $(-\pi, 0)$ and $(\pi, 2\pi)$

6. $(6x - 4)\sin x + (3x^2 - 4x)\cos x$

7. $\dfrac{4(5x-7x^3)\sec^2 x - 4(5-21x^2)\tan x}{(5x-7x^3)^2}$

8. $(\frac{\pi}{2}, \frac{\pi}{2})$ and $(\frac{5\pi}{2}, \frac{5\pi}{2})$

Derivatives. Exercise 8. Page 66-67.

1. $-2\sin(2x - 5)$

2. - 5.

3. $y = \dfrac{3}{2}(x - \pi) - 1$

140

4. $x = 0$, $\sqrt{\frac{\pi}{2}}$, $\sqrt{\frac{7\pi}{6}}$, $\sqrt{\frac{11\pi}{6}}$, $\sqrt{\frac{5\pi}{2}}$

5. $(160x^7 - 8 + 12\tan x \sec x)(5x^8 - 2x + 3\sec x)^3$

6. 0, $\frac{\pi}{2}$, π, $\frac{3\pi}{2}$, 2π **7.** -520

8. $y = 1040x - 2048$

9. $(8x\sin x + 4x^2 \cos x)\sec^2(4x^2 \sin x)$

10. $\cos x \tan(4x^2) + 8x \sin x \sec^2(4x^2)$

11. $\left(\frac{114}{(3x+5)^2}\right)\left(\frac{2x-3}{3x+5}\right)^5$ **12.** -151263

13. $-20x(7 - 2x)^4 \cos\left[(7 - 2x^2)^5\right]$

14. $y = -4.79699(x - 1) - .81081$

15. $\sin x \sin(\cos x)$ **16.** $\frac{-24x^2 - 24x - 16}{(4x^3 + 6x^2 + 8x + 9)^2}$

Derivatives. Exercise 9. Page 72-73.

1. $\frac{10x}{(\ln 3)(5x^2 + 1)}$

2. $10x \ln(5x^2 + 1) + 10x$

3. $4e^{4x-2}$

4. $\left[(2x + 3)(2x - \cos x) + (x^2 + 3x)(2 + \sin x)\right]$
   $e^{\left[(x^2 + 3x)(2x - \cos x)\right]}$

5. $\left(14x - 28 + \frac{42}{5-2x}\right)\left((x^2 - 4x - 3\ln(5 - 2x)\right)^6$

6. $\frac{-2\sec^2 x}{12 - 8\tan x} = \frac{\sec^2 x}{4\tan x - 6}$

7. $\frac{15\cos x - 60x^2}{3\sin x - 4x^3}$

8. $\frac{8 - 140x^9}{4x - 7x^{10}}$

9. $\frac{3x^2 + 8x^3 + 15x^4}{x^3 + 2x^4 + 3x^5} + \frac{\cos x - \sin x + \sec^2 x}{\sin x + \cos x + \tan x}$

10. $\frac{15\sqrt{x^3}}{2} - \frac{4}{x} + 10xe^{x^2}$

11. $\frac{-\frac{3}{x^2} - 2\sin x}{(\ln 5)(\frac{3}{x} + 2\cos x)}$ or $\frac{-3 - 2x^2 \sin x}{(\ln 5)(3x + 2x^2 \cos x)}$

12. $\frac{(8x-8)\cos(4x^2 - 8x)}{\sin(4x^2 - 8x)}$ or $(8x - 8)\cot(4x^2 - 8x)$

13. $(35x^4 - 4)(\ln 6)6^{7x^5 - 4x}$

14. $(280x^4 - 32)(7x^5 - 4x)^7 e^{(7x^5 - 4x)^8}$

15. $\frac{(6x - 8x^3)(8xe^{x^2} + 5\sec x \tan x) - (4e^{x^2} + 5\sec x)(6 - 24x^2)}{(6x - 8x^3)^2}$

16. $(4\sec^2 x - 10x^4)e^{4\tan x - 2x^5}$

17. $-3\sin x \cos^2 x e^{\cos^3 x}$

18. $(6x + 4\cos x - \frac{5}{8})e^{6x^4}$
   $+ 24x^3 e^{6x^4}(4x^2 + \sin x - \frac{5x}{8})$

19. $2\ln 4(\sec^2 x)4^{2\tan x}$

20. $\frac{6x}{3x^2 - 1} - \frac{4}{4x+1}$

21. $(-\frac{5}{2\sqrt{x}} + 4x - 17e^{17x})\sin(5\sqrt{x} - 2x^2 + e^{17x})$

22. $\frac{61}{(6x+5)^2}e^{\left(\frac{5x-6}{6x+5}\right)}$

23. $\frac{6x + 5 - (6x+5)\ln(3x^2 + 5x + 2)}{(3x^2 + 5x + 2)^2}$

24. 2

25. $(-1, -.0049575)$

26. First: $2e^{2x-15}$ Second: $4e^{2x-15}$
   Third: $8e^{2x-15}$ Tenth: $1024e^{2x-15}$

Derivatives. Exercise 10. Page 75.

1. $\left(\frac{12x+6}{x^2+x+1} + \frac{90x-40}{9x^2-8x+7} + \frac{24-60x^2+32x}{6x-5x^3+4x^2}\right)\left(x^2 + x + 1\right)^6$
   $\left(9x^2 - 8x + 7\right)^5\left(6x - 5x^3 + 4x^2\right)^4$

2. $\left(\frac{2x+1}{2x^2+2x+2} + \frac{90x-40}{9x^2-8x+7} - \frac{6-15x^2+8x}{6x-5x^3+4x^2}\right)$
   $\left(\frac{\sqrt{x^2+x+1}(9x^2-8x+7)^5}{6x-5x^3+4x^2}\right)$

3. $\left(\frac{18\sec x \tan x + 36\csc x \cot x - 54\csc^2 x}{\sec x - 2\csc x + 3\cot x} + \frac{18e^{3x} + 60x}{e^{3x} + 5x^2}\right.$
   $\left. - \frac{225x^4 - \frac{27}{x} + 54}{5x^5 - 3\ln x + 6x - 2}\right)$
   $\left(\frac{(\sec x - 2\csc x + 3\cot x)^{18}(e^{3x} + 5x^2)^6}{(5x^5 - 3\ln x + 6x - 2)^9}\right)$

4. $(1 + \ln x)x^x$

5. $(3\ln(\cos x) - (3x - 1)\tan x)(\cos x)^{3x-1}$

6. $\left(e^x \ln(\ln x) + \frac{e^x}{x\ln x}\right)(\ln x)^{e^x}$

7. $\left(\frac{2}{2x-1} - \frac{5}{5x+4}\right)\left(\frac{2x-1}{5x+4}\right)$
   $= \left(\frac{2(5x+4)-5(2x-1)}{(2x-1)(5x+4)}\right)\left(\frac{2x-1}{5x+4}\right)$
   $= \frac{13}{(5x+4)^2}$

8. $\left(\frac{2}{2x-1} + \frac{10}{5x+4}\right)(2x - 1)(5x + 4)^2$
   $= \left(\frac{2(5x+4)+10(2x-1)}{(2x-1)(5x+4)}\right)(2x - 1)(5x + 4)^2$
   $= (30x - 2)(5x + 4)$
   $= 150x^2 + 110x - 8$
   $= 2(5x + 4)^2 + 10(2x - 1)(5x + 4)$

Derivatives. Exercise 11. Page 77.

1. $(e^7 \cos t)(3t^8 - \frac{1}{t}) + (e^7 \sin t)(24t^7 + \frac{1}{t^2})$

2. e^t **3.** $t^{\frac{1}{t}}\left(\frac{1 - \ln t}{t^2}\right)$

4. $32t^7 - \frac{15}{4}t^{-\frac{1}{4}} + \frac{14}{t^3} + \frac{8}{3\sqrt[3]{t^2}}$

141

5. $-24t^5 \sin(4t^6)$

6. $-24 \sin t \cos^5 t$

7. $\frac{6t+5}{\ln 4(3t^2+5t)}$

8. $\frac{(\sec^2 t)(14t-6)-14\tan t}{(14t-6)^2}$

9. $12t^3 e^{(3t^4 - \ln 7)}$

10. 0

11. $2\cot(2t)\csc(2t)$

12. $(\ln 4)(\sec t)(\tan t)4^{\sec t}$

13. $\ln 8$

14. $4(\sec 4t)(\tan 4t)$

15. $(\ln(\log_5 6))(\log_5 6)^t$

16. $\frac{6}{t}$

17. $\csc^2 t$

18. $\frac{1}{(\ln 17)t}$

19. $-12t^2$

20. $e^t - 12t^2$

21. $-\sin t + \frac{12}{t^4}$

22. $\frac{25t^4 + e^t}{5t^5 + e^t}$

23. $\frac{4}{5\sqrt[5]{t^4}}$

24. $\frac{1}{t} + \frac{4}{5\sqrt[5]{t^4}}$

25. $(e)\cos(et)$

26. $\frac{e}{t}$

27. $440(2t-7)^{54}$

28. $\sqrt{7}\sec^2\left(\sqrt{7}t\right)$

29. $18(e^t - \frac{1}{t})(e^t - \ln t)^{17}$

30. $\frac{-38}{(5t+6)^2}\sin\left(\frac{3t-4}{5t+6}\right)$

31. $\frac{-3\sin t(5t+6)-5(3\cos t-4)}{(5t+6)^2}$

32. $7(t + \sin^5(3t^4 + 10t - 2))^6$

$(1 + 5(12t^3 + 10)\cos(3t^4 + 10t - 2)$

$\sin^4(3t^4 + 10t - 2))$

Derivatives. Exercise 12. Page 80-81.

1. $\frac{x}{y}$

2. $\frac{2x}{1-2y}$

3. -1

4. 6

5. $y = \frac{-13}{8}x + \frac{3}{8}$

6. $(0,-5)$ and $(0,5)$

7. $(-3,0)$ and $(3,0)$

8. $\frac{30}{7}$

Derivatives. Exercise 13. Page 83.

1. $\frac{1}{\sqrt{1-x^2}}$

2. $\frac{-1}{\sqrt{1-x^2}}$

3. $\frac{1}{|x|\sqrt{x^2-1}}$

4. $\frac{-1}{|x|\sqrt{x^2-1}}$

5. $\frac{-1}{1+x^2}$

6. $\frac{1}{18}$

7. $-\frac{1}{2}$

8. $-\frac{1}{2}$

Appl. of Derivatives. Exercise 1. Page 86.

1. Not differentiable at 0.
Not continuous and not differentiable at 5.

2. Not differentiable at 0.
Not continuous and not differentiable at 4.

3. Not differentiable at 4.
Not continuous and not differentiable at 5.

4. Not continuous and not differentiable at 4.
Not differentiable at 5.

5. Not continuous and not differentiable at 0.
Not differentiable at 5.

6. Not continuous and not differentiable at 0.
Not differentiable at 4.

7. Not differentiable at -3.
Not continuous and not differentiable at 5.

8. Not continuous and not differentiable at 4.
Not differentiable at 6.

Appl. of Derivatives. Exercise 2. Page 89.

1. $-\frac{1}{6}$

2. 0

3. undefined

4. $\frac{2}{3}$

5. 0

6. $-\frac{\pi}{2}$

7. $\frac{1}{3}$

8. undefined

9. undefined

10. $-\frac{2}{3}$

Appl. of Derivatives. Exercise 3. Page 98.

1. relative minimum at -9.
relative maximum at 0.
relative and absolute minimum at 15.

2. relative maximum at $-\sqrt{3}$.
relative minimum at $\sqrt{3}$.

3. relative minimum at -3.
relative maximum at $\frac{-1-\sqrt{5}}{2}$.
relative and absolute minimum at $\frac{-1+\sqrt{5}}{2}$.

4. endpoint maximum at $\frac{1}{2}$.
relative and absolute minimum at 1.
endpoint and absolute maximum at 2.

5. relative maximum at 1.

6. relative and absolute maximum at 0.
endpoint and absolute minimum at $-\frac{7}{3}$.
endpoint and absolute minimum at $\frac{7}{3}$.

7. relative and absolute maximum at 0.

8. endpoint minimum at $-\pi$.
relative maximum at $-\frac{5\pi}{6}$.
relative and absolute minimum at $-\frac{\pi}{6}$.
endpoint and absolute maximum at π.

9. relative maximum at $-\frac{5\pi}{6}$.
relative and absolute minimum at $-\frac{\pi}{6}$.

10. endpoint and absolute minimum at 0.
relative and absolute maximum at $\frac{1}{2}$.

11. no extrema of any kind.

12. endpoint minimum at 0.

absolute and relative maximum at $\frac{\pi}{6}$.

relative minimum at $\frac{\pi}{2}$.

absolute and relative maximum at $\frac{5\pi}{6}$.

absolute and relative minimum at $\frac{3\pi}{2}$.

endpoint maximum at 2π.

Appl. of Derivatives. Exercise 4. Page 106.

1.
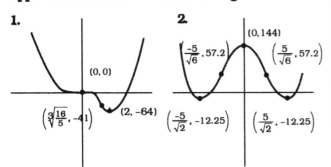

2
(0, 144), $\left(\frac{-5}{\sqrt{6}}, 57.2\right)$, $\left(\frac{5}{\sqrt{6}}, 57.2\right)$, $\left(\frac{-5}{\sqrt{2}}, -12.25\right)$, $\left(\frac{5}{\sqrt{2}}, -12.25\right)$

3.
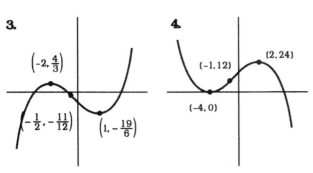

4.

5.
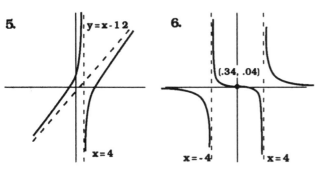

6.

7.
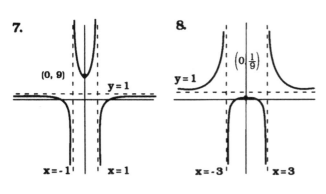

8.

9.
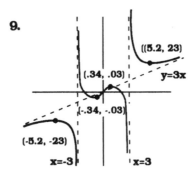

10.
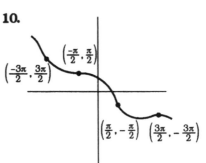

11.
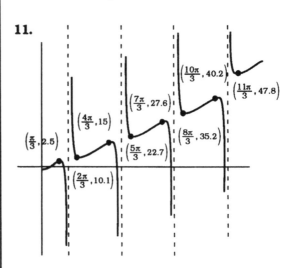

12.
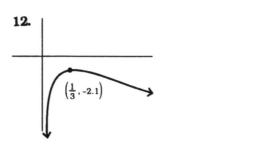

Appl. of Derivatives. Exercise 5. Page 110.

1. 1.22 (actual value 1.26)

2 4.26 (actual value 4.26)

3. 1.0901 (actual value 1.0960)

4. 0.06283 (actual value 0.06279)

Appl. of Derivatives. Exercise 5. Page 110 (con't)

5. -0.17 (actual value -0.186)

6. 2.00375 (actual value 2.003736)

7. $.24\sqrt{3}$, or 0.4157

8. 12π, or 37.7

Appl. of Derivatives. Exercise 6. Page 113.

1. 6.657967005

2. -1.375927985

3. 0.9210245497

4. 8.653311931

5. -1.371134331

6. 10.33559363

7. -2.875699523

8. -0.6058295862

Appl. of Derivatives. Exercise 7. Page 119-120.

1. 78x104

2. 41, 41

3. 41, 41

4. 28x28x14

5. 6912

6. r=1.2, h=2.4

7. (-1, -1)

8. Use 12 inches for the square and 3π inches for the circle.

9. 14x14x28

10. 6 thousand

Appl. of Derivatives. Exercise 8. Page 123-124.

1. r=9, x=9

2. r=7.377, x=13.172

3. r=10.23, x=0

4. $5\sqrt{5}$, or 11.18 ft.

5. 728.5 yd.

6. 2 ft.

7. 15 miles from point A, 27 miles from B.

8. 338 sq. in.

Appl. of Derivatives. Exercise 9. Page 128-129.

1. (0, 4) and (12, ∞)

2. $\left(\frac{3}{2}, 3\right)$ and $\left(\frac{9}{2}, 6\right)$

3. a. t=4
   b. 2.39

4. a. 8
   b. opposite
   c. $\frac{3}{2}$
   d. (0, 4)

5. 240 ft.

6. 32 ft. per sec.

7. 120 ft. per sec.

8. 68 ft.

Appl. of Derivatives. Exercise 10. Page 133-134.

1. 6π ft.^{2}/sec.

2. 271.2 ft.^{3}/min.

3. $\frac{4}{3}$ ft./sec.

4. 18 ft./sec.

5. -30 units/minute

6. -29.9 units/minute

7. 10.087 km./hr.

8. -3.88

Appl. of Derivatives. Exercise 11. Page 136.

1. There are eight possible answers:
$\frac{\pi}{2}, \frac{3\pi}{2}, \frac{5\pi}{2}, \frac{7\pi}{2}, \frac{9\pi}{2}, \frac{11\pi}{2}, \frac{13\pi}{2}, \frac{15\pi}{2}$.

2. No such c exists; the function is not continuous at $x=\frac{\pi}{2}$.

3. No such c exists; the function is not continuous at x=0.

4. If f(x) has two different zeros, then Rolle's Theorem says that there will be a c between the two zeros, for which f'(c) =0. However, f'(x), which is $3x^2+6x+9$, has no zeros.

5. 1.266

6. No such c exists; f(x) is not differentiable at x=-2.

7. 0.772

8. Point (0, 1), tangent line y=x+1.

ENGLISH SERIES

The **Straight Forward English** series is designed to measure, teach, review, and master specific English skills. All pages are reproducible and include answers to exercises and tests.

Capitalization & Punctuation
GP-032 • 40 pages

I and First Words; Proper Nouns; Ending Marks and Sentences; Commas; Apostrophes; Quotation Marks.

Nouns & Pronouns
GP-033 • 40 pages

Singular and Plural Nouns; Common and Proper Nouns; Concrete and Abstract Nouns; Collective Nouns; Possessive Pronouns; Pronouns and Contractions; Subject and Object Pronouns.

Verbs
GP-034 • 40 pages

Action Verbs; Linking Verbs; Verb Tense; Subject-Verb Agreement; Spelling Rules for Tense; Helping Verbs; Irregular Verbs; Past Participles.

Sentences
GP-041 • 40 pages

Sentences; Subject and Predicate; Sentence Structures.

Adjectives & Adverbs
GP-035 • 40 pages

Proper Adjectives; Articles; Demonstrative Adjectives; Comparative Adjectives; Special Adjectives: Good and Bad; -ly Adverbs; Comparative Adverbs; Good-Well and Bad-Badly.

Prepositions, Conjunctions and Interjections
GP-043 • 40 pages

Recognizing Prepositions; Object of the Preposition; Prepositional Phrases; Prepositional Phrases as Adjectives and Adverbs; Faulty Reference; Coordinating, Correlative and Subordinate Conjunctions.

ADVANCED ENGLISH SERIES

Get It Right!
GP-148 • 144 pages

Organized into four sections, **Get It Right!** is designed to teach writing skills commonly addressed in the standardized testing in the early grades: Spelling, Mechanics, Usage, and Proofreading. Overall the book includes 100 lessons, plus reviews and skill checks.

All-In-One English
GP-107 • 112 pages

The **All-In-One** is a master book to the Straight Forward English Series.
Under one cover it has included the important English skills of capitalization, punctuation, and all eight parts of speech. Each selection of the All-In-One explains and models a skill and then provides focused practice, periodic review, and testing to help measure acquired skills. Progress through all skills is thorough and complete.

Grammar Rules!
GP-102 • 250 pages

Grammar Rules! is a straightforward approach to basic English grammar and English writing skills. Forty units each composed of four lessons for a total of 160 lessons, plus review, skill checks, and answers. Units build skills with Parts of Speech, Mechanics, Diagramming, and Proofreading. Solid grammar and writing skills are explained, modeled, practiced, reviewed, and tested.

Clauses & Phrases
GP-055 • 80 pages

Adverb, Adjective and Noun Clauses; Gerund, Participial and Infinitive Verbals; Gerund, Participial, Infinitive, Prepositional and Appositive Phrases.

Mechanics
GP-056 • 80 pages

Abbreviations; Apostrophes; Capitalization; Italics; Quotation Marks; Numbers; Commas; Semicolons; Colons; Hyphens; Parentheses; Dashes; Brackets; Ellipses; Slashes.

Grammar & Diagramming Sentences
GP-075 • 110 pages

The Basics; Diagramming Rules and Patterns; Nouns and Pronouns; Verbs; Modifiers; Prepositions, Conjunctions, and Special Items; Clauses and Compound-Complex Sentences.

Troublesome Grammar
GP-019 • 120 pages •

Agreement; Regular and Irregular Verbs; Modifiers; Prepositions and Case, Possessives and Contractions; Plurals; Active and Passive Voice; Comparative Forms; Word Usage; and more.

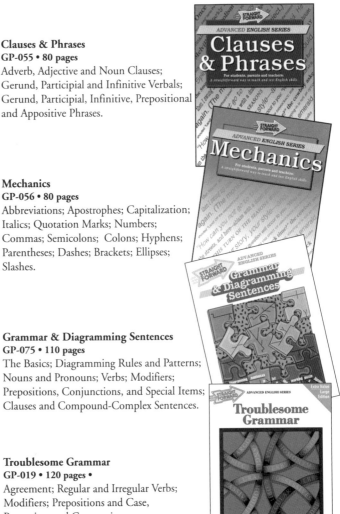

Math Series

The Straight Forward Math Series

is systematic, first diagnosing skill levels, then *practice*, periodic *review*, and *testing*.

Blackline

GP-006 Addition
GP-012 Subtraction
GP-007 Multiplication
GP-013 Division
GP-039 Fractions
GP-083 Word Problems, Book 1
GP-042 Word Problems, Book 2

GarlicPress
Tools for Learning and Growing

The Advanced Straight Forward Math Series

is a higher level system to diagnose, practice, review, and test skills.

Blackline

GP-015 Advanced Addition
GP-016 Advanced Subtraction
GP-017 Advanced Multiplication
GP-018 Advanced Division
GP-020 Advanced Decimals
GP-021 Advanced Fractions
GP-044 Mastery Tests
GP-025 Percent
GP-028 Pre-Algebra, Book 1
GP-029 Pre-Algebra, Book 2
GP-030 Pre-Geometry, Book 1
GP-031 Pre-Geometry, Book 2
GP-163 Pre-Algebra Companion

Upper Level Math Series

GP-104 Algebra, Book 1
GP-105 Algebra, Book 2
GP-045 Trigonometry
GP-054 Geometry
GP-053 Pre-Calculus
GP-064 Calculus AB, Vol. 1
GP-067 Calculus AB, Vol. 2

Math Pyramid Puzzles

Math Pyramid Puzzles
ISBN 978-1-9308-2062-3
GP-162
5 two-sided puzzles

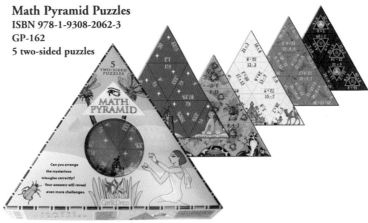

Assemble 5 two-sided puzzles each with different mathematical challenges. Solve the mathematical pyramid on the front side, turn the clear tray over to reveal of problem of logic: percents, decimals, fractions, exponents and factors.

Start building your pyramid at the bottom. The center piece is labeled and the picture may offer a clue.

Use your math skills to match sides with the same value.

You may find more than one match, but **all sides that touch** must match. When you are satisfied with your solution, close the tray.

Turn over and check the back. If the pieces are in order, you are correct!

Now, can you solve this logic puzzle?